GOOD VICTORY

GOOD VICTORY

Metropolitan Orestes Chornock
and the American Carpatho-Russian
Orthodox Greek Catholic Diocese

by

Lawrence Barriger

Holy Cross Orthodox Press
Brookline, Massachusetts 02146

Published by Holy Cross Orthodox Press
50 Goddard Avenue
Brookline, Massachusetts 02146

Cover design by Mary C. Vaporis

Library of Congress Cataloging-in-Publication Data

Barriger, Lawrence.
Metropolitan Orestes Chornock and the American
Carpatho-Russian Orthodox Greek Catholic Diocese.
Bibliography: p.
1. Chornock, Orestes P. 2. American Carpatho-Russian Or-
thodox Greek Catholic Diocese in U.S.A.—Bishops—Biography.
3. Orthodox Eastern Church—United States—Bishops—
Biography. I. Title.
BX738.A69C483 1985   281.9'3   85-17678
ISBN 0-917651-13-8

Contents

Office of the Bishop
312 Garfield St., Johnstown, Pa. 15906

PREFACE

A century has passed since the birth of our illustrious Metropolitan Orestes, and the legacy which he has bequeathed to us is just as fresh and wholesome as the day he was born.

It is appropriate that we, his spiritual heirs, fittingly call to remembrance his spiritual qualities and pay tribute to his multitude of efforts on behalf of our Diocese. He was a hierarch who overcame countless obstacles in defending his flock. His episcopacy among us is held up for our emulation as an example of a loving and concerned father. He exalted by his life and devotion the episcopal office. All that our Diocese has become, we can firmly attribute to his ideals and vision and the foundation in Christ which he established for us.

In reading these collected pages of GOOD VICTORY, which was derived from his coat of arms, I am pleased with the honest and worthwhile presentation of his life. We need heroes whose example we might emulate. We need to recall the tremendous personal sacrifices he made for us. We must call to mind his heroism and courage. He was indeed a man among men, a priest's priest and a Bishop's Bishop.

There are very few of our Faith who had the good fortune to know him who today cannot recall pleasant and holy memories in his presence. For this reason, we are indebted to our National ACRY which commissioned the publication of this worthy book, so that our younger generation can become acquainted with this man of God and pursue his ideals of Christian Orthodoxy.

Just as Our Lord directed the vision of the Chosen Twelve far beyond the confines of the Plain, far beyond the lofty heights of Mount Hermon, so our founding father urged us to see beyond ourselves and our limitations and to open ourselves to the Grace of the Holy Spirit, to where He would lead us, so that we might achieve our rightful destiny in God's Providence. Our holy duty and sacred obligation is to pursue with the same perseverance and devotion the task of salvation for ourselves and for others as did our beloved Metropolitan Orestes.

The American Carpatho-Russian Orthodox Greek Catholic Diocese of the U.S.A.

It should be a joyous task to peruse and read carefully the life of our first Diocesan Bishop and to glean from its soulful insights of the man as a priest, father and Bishop. He represents for us a man plagued by insurmountable problems and even personal deficiencies, who found in the Grace of God the strength to rise beyond them and lead us back in our pilgrimage to our ancestral Orthodox Faith.

It pleases me to heartily recommend this publication to all who are interested in the study of our beloved people and their history in the United States, because embodied in the life of the Metropolitan are all these and more. I commend Father Lawrence Barriger for his insightful labor of love and thorough research. This text should be read and re-read again to achieve its goal in our midst.

With my episcopal blessing,

+ N I C H O L A S
Bishop of the Diocese

The American Carpatho-Russian Orthodox Greek Catholic Diocese of the U.S.A.

Glory Be To Jesus Christ!

Dear Reader:

On September 5, 1981, Chapter 43 of Rockaway, NJ, proposed to the delegates of the 37th National ACRY Convention, that an honorarium be set up to produce a biography of Metropolitan Orestes, of Blessed Memory. The delegates that had convened that day overwhelmingly agreed that the life of our Founding Father and Supreme Patron should be truthfully recorded so that future generations might look back and discover their "Roots".

His Excellency Bishop John Martin, of Blessed Memory, was asked by the membership to recommend and to appoint an appropriate person to research and write the biography. At the 38th National Convention, His Excellency announced that he had appointed Fr. Lawrence Barriger to complete this task.

After Fr. Barriger's manuscript was well under way, it became clear to the membership that a large amount of money was needed to complete this project. After studying several different suggestions to raise the necessary funds, the delegates of the 39th National Convention initiated the "Metropolitan Orestes Biography Bowl-A-Thon". In one short year, the entire sum needed was raised by the members throughout our dioceses.

Now, as the end of one phase of a **Good Victory's** journey is in sight, it is time to pause and pay honor to some of those who gave credibility and stability to this project:

To His Grace, Bishop Nicholas, who gave his support and counsel;
To His Excellency Bishop John, whose wisdom and guidance gave us a talented author;
To past National President Emil Mischiko, who nursed this project through its early days;
To National Sr. Spiritual Advisor, Rev. Fr. Frank Miloro, whose spiritual advice and support to all involved gave us strength;
To National Vice-President Mary Kay Wanchik, whose expertise was invaluable in working with the publisher;
A special thanks to all of the members of the ACRY and to our diocesan families who so generously contributed to this project;
And especially to Rev. Fr. Lawrence Barriger, who literally donated three years of his life so that we might all enjoy a **Good Victory.**

Yours In The Lord,

Michele A. Tomko

Michele A. Tomko
National President

May 1, 1985

Member of COUNCIL *of* EASTERN ORTHODOX YOUTH LEADERS *of the* AMERICAS

Author's Forward

In the summer of 1982, His Excellency, the late Bishop John asked me to undertake for the National A.C.R.Y. the task of gathering research materials and preparing a biography of Metropolitan Orestes, the founding bishop of our American Carpatho-Russian Orthodox Diocese. I knew that this would be a great task, as much of needed information was quite literally lying about in old newspapers, journals, Sobor minutes, commemorative books and other sources that for the most part were completely without any sort of index or guide as to contents.

The few books and articles that have been written about the so-called "celibacy struggle" of the 1930s either lack detail, or seek to present Metropolitan Orestes and the other founders of our diocese as rebellious and deceptive priests, or both. The evidence that I have gathered and presented in these pages shows that is a false portrait.

Metropolitan Orestes was a remarkable man, and the 1936 description of him as a priest after the heart of Christ is, after assessing his struggles, his "podvih" from the Unia back to the Orthodox Faith and the trials that awaited him even in the bosom of Orthodoxy, an accurate description.

There are many people who remember Metropolitan Orestes and the early days of the diocese still but every year their number grows smaller and there are a growing group of people who are perhaps unaware of the meaning of his life. In undertaking this work my appreciation of the Metropolitan and those heroic priests and faithful who struggled with him was greatly renewed. It is my hope that those who read these pages, both young and old, will come to share in that renewed appreciation with me.

To the members of the A.C.R.Y. who suggested the writing of this book and who financed it I would like to say "Thank You" for giving me the opportunity to learn and discover for myself the "Good Victory" of Metropolitan Orestes.

Great Lent, 1985
Fr. Lawrence Barriger

Acknowledgements

There are several remarkable individuals that I must acknowledge; without their kind help and guidance this book could simply not have been undertaken:

The late Bishop John Martin, who not only assigned me the task of writing this book, but who spent many hours giving me a perspective on events, something he, as the former chancellor of the Byzantine Catholic jurisdiction and, after embracing Orthodoxy, the bishop who succeeded the Metropolitan, was uniquely qualified to do.

The Rt. Rev. Mitred E. Molchany, the Vicar-General of our diocese since 1938 and pastor of St. Nicholas Orthodox Greek Catholic Church of Homestead, the last of the "founding fathers" of our diocese. Fr. Vicar shared a memorable afternoon with me reflecting on the "Bor'ba" and the early days of our diocese. He provided many insights into people and the events of the '30s and '40s.

The Very Rev. Protopresbyter John Yurcisin, dean of our Christ the Saviour Cathedral in Johnstown, Pa. and diocesan chancellor, who provided me with valuable materials from the diocesan archives and answers to my many questions on the background of the incidents and people that I encountered in those materials.

The Very Rev. James S. Dutko, editor of *The Church Messenger* and rector of our Christ the Saviour Seminary, who not only suggested the title of the book but also provided me with a room at the Seminary where all of the research and most of the writing of this book took place.

The Very Rev. Michael G. Dahulich, vice-chancellor of the diocese and secretary to the bishop, who gave critical advice on the first chapters of the book and who offered many suggestions towards its completion.

Mr. John Kamenitsky of St. John the Baptist Canonical Orthodox Church of Stratford, Conn. Mr. Kamenitsky knew the Metropolitan since the 1914 and provided many insights into church life at Arctic Street, Mill Hill Avenue, Broadbridge Avenue and Silver Lane. He was a close friend of the Metropolitan, especially in the later years of the Metropolitan's life.

Mr. John Kamenitsky, past National A.C.R.Y. president, who likewise, with his father, provided many insights into the events of the Metropolitan's life in Bridgeport and Stratford. They were kind enough to speak with me far into the night one summer evening in Stratford.

The many people who shared their remembrances of the Metropolitan with me, gave me photographs, and otherwise encouraged my work. It was not possible of course to use every photograph or every story but all of them helped to give me a vision of the man. Although I had met Metropolitan Orestes on several occasions as a young Seminarian, I did not know him personally and every shared memory helped me to come to "know" him.

Fr. N. Michael Vaporis and his staff at the Holy Cross Orthodox Press, who were kind enough to undertake the actual composition and printing of the book.

And last, but certainly not least, my wife Linda and daughter Laura Elizabeth, who sacrificed a husband and a father with understanding for the many long hours that the researching and writing of this book took.

All who undertake a study of the 1930s and the early history of the Carpatho-Russian people and their churches in America will owe a special debt of gratitude to the Rev. John Slivka of Brooklyn, New York for his anthology of documents and primary texts pertinent of the era entitled *Historical Mirror: Sources of the Russian and Hungarian Greek Catholics in the United States of America* (Brooklyn, N.Y., 1978). His work was a most useful reference tool.

Abbreviations and Terms Used

A R V   *The Amerikanskij Russkij Viestnik (Russian American Messenger)*—the official newspaper of the Greek Catholic Union of Russian Brotherhoods.

G C U   The Greek Catholic Union of Russian Brotherhoods (Sojedinenije) sometimes referred to as the "Greek Catholic Union".

Vistnik   *(Messenger).* The first newspaper of the American Carpatho-Russian Orthodox Greek Catholic Diocese, from 1936-1946. After 1946, it was published by Fr. Stephen Varzaly of Rankin, Pa.

The Church Messenger   *(Cerkovnyj Viestnik)* the current (1946 to present) newspaper of the American Carpatho-Russian Orthodox Greek Catholic Diocese.

Viestnik   A reference to the A R V. The newspapers of the Carpatho-Russian communities can be quite confusing; everyone liked the name "Viestnik"—"Messenger" as the name of their paper. There were even others besides these three. I have referred to *The Church Messenger* by its English name to further distinguish it from the other two mentioned.

Prjasevska
Rus'   The area where Carpatho-Russians lived
            about the city of Prjasev, (Russian), also
            known in Slovak as Presov and in Hungarian
            as Eperjes. The city of Uzhorod is also called
            by its Hungarian name of Ungvar and
            Muchachevo is also known by some authors
            as Munkacs.

Ruthenian   The term used by the Vatican for Carpatho-
            Russians. Rusyn and Carpatho-Rusyn are
            also used to refer to Carpatho-Russians as is
            the term Uhro-Rusyn (or Uhro-Russian for
            "Hungarian Russian," i.e. Russians who lived
            in Hungary).

Uniate   (United) A term used primarily by Orthodox
            to refer to members of the "Byzantine" or
            other "Eastern Rite" Roman Catholic Church.

List of Photographs

elect of an Orthodox Carpatho-Russian Diocese.

Following p. 134:

17. First Class of the Diocesan Seminary in New York City in 1940, shown with Bishop Orestes.

18. Masthead of *Vistnik*, volume 1, number 1.

Following p. 149:

19. Fr. Stephen Varzaly.

20. Front page of *Cerkovnyj Viestnik: The Church Messenger*, vol. 1, no. 1, 1946.

21. Ecumenical Patriarch Benjamin I.

22. Bishop Orestes and Patriarch Athenagoras.

Following p. 160:

23. Christ the Saviour Cathedral, Johnstown, Pa. The Mother Church and Spiritual Center of the American Carpatho-Russian Orthodox Greek Catholic Diocese.

24. The original Christ the Saviour Seminary building, 1951.

25. Scenes from the dedication of the Cathedral, 1954.

26. Scenes from the dedication of the Cathedral, 1954.

Following page 166:

27. Bishop Peter Shymansky (1963-1964).

28. Bishop Methodios Kanchuha (1965).

29. Metropolitan Orestes bestowing the rank of Archimandrite upon Fr. John Martin prior to his consecration as bishop on September 4, 1966 at old St. George's Church, Taylor, Pa.

30. Bishop John Martin (1966-1984).

31. The new Diocesan Administration Building and Bishop's Residence.

32. Liturgy in the Cathedral.

Following p. 171:

33. His Eminence, the Most Reverend Orestes P. Chornock, D.D., Titular Metropolitan of Agathonikeia, Bishop

of the American Carpatho-Russian Orthodox Greek Catholic Diocese.

34. His Eminence Metropolitan Orestes with the Most Reverend John R. Martin, D.D., Titular Bishop of Nyssa and Auxiliary Bishop of the Diocese.

35. "Lord, O Lord, look down from heaven and see, and visit and bless his vineyard . . ."

36. Bishop Orestes on his Golden Anniversary

Chapter 1

BEGINNINGS

In the year A.D. 303, the Roman Emperor Diocletian wished to consolidate and strengthen his authority over the many different nations and cultures to be found in the borders of his rule. To this aim he believed that a return to the old pagan Roman religion, with its rituals and sacrifices, would foster unity and break down any cultural aspirations of his subject people. Of the many religious groups in his empire the people who were called Christians were notorious for refusing to practice the "official" religion of the empire and clung to their faith. In order to deal with Christians, Emperor Diocletian ordered them persecuted and their churches destroyed.[1]

In the course of the persecution, a physician of Tyana, in Cappadocia (present day Turkey), refused to renounce the belief in Jesus Christ and to offer sacrifice to the idols prescribed by the emperor. The physician's confession of faith led to his martyrdom and the wild horses which pulled his body apart sealed it in blood. His name was Orestes.[2]

On the 11th day of July 1883, the village of Ortutova, in the Austro-Hungarian county of Saris, Prjasevska Rus', word spread among the villagers that Pani Mary, the wife of their beloved pastor, Fr. John Chornock, had just given birth to their second child. His name was Orestes.[3]

Young Orestes attended elementary school some ten miles from his home in Ortutova in the town of Bardejov, Saris county, in the years 1889 to 1894. Having completed his elementary education, he attended the Royal Gymnasium of Presov, which he graduated from with honors in 1902.

In Carpatho-Russia at the turn of the century, life was centered on and about the village church, and the priesthood was seen as being one of the highest possible goals for a young man to aspire to. Having heard the inner call of the Holy Spirit to continue the work of Christ on earth, Orestes did not delay in answering, and the fall of 1902 found him enrolled as a student in the Presov Theological Academy. An exemplary student and seminarian, with a special love for the ritual and music of his church, he completed his theological studies and, at the age of twenty-three, became a candidate for ordination.

According to the tradition of the Church, seminarians must marry before ordination (unless they choose not to marry at all). On July 17, 1906, Orestes Chornock was accordingly united with Yolanda Molchany, the twenty-one year old daughter of the Rev. Vladimir and Pani Bertha Molchany, in the sacrament of Holy Matrimony.

On the feast of the Falling Asleep of the Mother of God, August 28, 1906, Deacon Orestes Chornock was ordained to the priesthood by the Most Rev. Dr. John Valyi, the bishop of the diocese of Presov. The ordination took place in the Presov Cathedral and the new priest was assigned to serve as the pastor of the village of Osturna, the westernmost Carpatho-Russian village in Europe, a Carpatho-Russian island surrounded by an ethnic sea which contained Slovaks, Germans, Poles, Czechs, and Hungarians, not to mention Gypsies and Jews.

Karpatska Rus'

The area known as *Karpatska Rus'*, "Carpatho-Russia," is today divided. A large part has been annexed by the Soviet Union and is known as the Pod Karpatska Oblast' of the Soviet Republic of the Ukraine. Another part, Prjasevska Rus' is a part of eastern Slovakia in Czechoslovakia. A third part is now a part of Hungary. The area on the southern side of the Carpathian Mountains is known as *Pod Karpatska Rus'* or Sub Carpatho-Russia. The northern side is known as *Pri-Karpatska Rus'* or "Near" (i.e."close") Carpatho-Russia or more commonly as Galicia. Today this area is divided between Poland and the Soviet Ukraine.

Karpatska Rus' never existed as an independent country.[4] The name *Rus'* was the name given to the lands inhabited by the eastern Slavs. At the time of Prince Vladimir at the end of the tenth century, *Karpatska Rus'* became a part of the greater kingdom of *Cervenna Rus'*, "Red Russia," which was ruled by Vladimir and his descendants from the city of Kiev. The name Rus' in the eleventh and twelfth centuries came to mean all of the territory ruled by the Russian princes and their populations.[5]

In the eleventh and twelfth century Kiev and Kievan Russia were subject to constant raids from nomadic Asian tribes. Many of its citizens left and took refuge in Galician Russia making it by the twelfth century one of the strongest and most important Russian principalities. The Galician Russian kingdom, weakened by the attack of the Tartars under Batu Khan in 1241, an attack that spilled over the Carpathian Mountains into Hungary, became divided due to internal dissent. It was later taken by the Poles in 1340.

However, before this time *Karpatska Rus'* had already fallen under the rule of the Hungarian kings. The Galician princes had problems ruling *Karpatska Rus'* because it was on the other side of the high Carpathian Mountains. The Hungarian King Kalomon in 1099 attempted to seize *Karpatska Rus'* but was defeated by the Galician Russian Prince Volodar Rastislavich of Peremysl.[6] At the end of the twelfth century the Hungarians were able to incorporate *Karpatska Rus'* into their territory without interference from the Galician princes on the northern side of the Carpathians. The princes were involved in internal disputes and were either unable or unwilling to respond to their encroachment. The Carpatho-Russian people were to remain from that time until 1918 one of the many subject peoples of the Hungarian nation.[7]

Christianity in Karpatska Rus'

The Carpatho-Russian people themselves trace their conversion to Christianity to the mission of Cyril and Methodios, which was commissioned by one of the greatest patriarchs of Constantinople, Saint Photios. Saints Cyril and Methodios were sent at the request of Prince Rastislav of Moravia in the year 862. The mission of Saints Cyril and Methodios used the vernacular Slavonic language, something revolutionary in the Middle Ages and something that brought them into conflict with the Latin missions in the area, which were supported by neighboring German bishops under the jurisdiction of the pope of Rome. Cyril responded to the Roman claims that only the "languages of the Cross," that is, Greek, Latin and Hebrew could be used in liturgical worship by saying, "To conduct the Divine Services in a language not known by the people is like writing on sand: it could not bear any spiritual fruit."[8]

In an attempt to overcome the resistance of the Latin missionaries, Cyril and Methodios journeyed to Rome to seek the assistance of the Pope.[9] Cyril died in Rome, but

4

Methodios returned to his work among the Slavs in Moravia with the blessing of Pope Adrian II. Methodios worked to establish the archdiocese of Moravia and Panonia in the face of continuing opposition from the Latin clergy until his death in 885. If the disciples of Cyril and Methodios followed the ninth century Moravian sphere of influence, it is conceivable that they could have reached as far as Peremysl in Galicia.[10]

The missionary activity in the Moravian Empire, which encompassed Moravia, northern Hungary, and part of *Karpatska Rus'*, resulted in the establishment of seven dioceses which made up the archdiocese of Saint Methodios.[11] While the names of six of the seven are known, the seventh one remains a mystery. Since the Carpatho-Russian area was not a part of the terrritory of any of the six known bishops, the Carpatho-Russians believed that the seventh diocese was located in Carpatho-Russia and that the town of Mukachevo was the see of its bishop.

Although not long after the death of Methodios, the successors of Rastislav began to work for the destruction of the Slavonic Liturgy and the incorporation of Moravia and Panonia into the fold of the German bishops. There is evidence that the Slavonic Liturgy was not completely displaced by the Latin one, but continued to survive among the western Slavs.[12] The Benedictine Abbey of Sazava, founded by Saint Prokopios in 1032 in Bohemia, not only celebrated its Divine Liturgy and offices in Slavonic, but also had contacts with Kiev.[13]

In time, however, the Latin language and the Roman Liturgy replaced the Slavonic Liturgy of Cyril and Methodios among the western Slavs, and today the Slovaks, Czechs, and Poles, all are members of the Roman Church and, until recently, were forbidden the use of any other liturgical language than Latin.

The earliest records relating to church life in Carpatho-Russia date from the fourteenth century. At that time the parishes of Prjasevska Rus' were under the Orthodox bishop of Peremysl in Galicia.[14] In 1491, an Orthodox bishop was appointed by the Hungarian king for the town of Muchachevo, and the churches of Prjasevska Rus' fell under his jurisdiction, although close ties were maintained between the dioceses of Muchachevo and Peremysl. Both of these dioceses, like the others in all of the lands of *Rus'*, were subject to the metropolitan of Kiev, who entered under the direct jurisdiction of the patriarch of Constantinople.[15]

Monasticism in Carpatho-Russia

It has been said that Orthodox monasticism is a barometer of spiritual life. The tenth to the fourteenth century was a time of renewal and development in Orthodox monasticism. The monasteries on Athos have their beginnings in this period. It was at this time that the Monastery of the Caves in Kiev, the *Kievo-Pecerskja Lavra*, was founded by Saint Anthony (1073) and strengthened by his successor as abbot, Saint Theodosios (1074). Monks from Carpatho-Russia lived at Mount Athos and at the Monastery of the Caves in Kiev. One of them, Moses Uhrin (1043), became one of the earliest saints of the monastery.[16]

The monastic traditions found on Mount Athos and especially at the Monastery of the Caves were brought back by monks to *Karpatska Rus'*. The memory of Saint Athanasios of Mount Athos (1009) was kept on the church calendar even after the Orthodox faith was abolished and the intercession of Anthony and Theodosios "of the Caves," *Pecerskich*, was asked for by Carpatho-Russians in their prayers from an early date. The purely Orthodox ceremony of the *Panagia* continued to be used even after the monasteries of *Karpatska Rus'* were turned over to Roman Catholic "Basilian" monks.[17]

Orthodox monasteries were quite numerous in *Karpatska Rus'*, the monks were valued as spiritual fathers, and pilgrimages to monasteries were quite popular. Monasteries

6

were found in Levosa, Legnava, Pazdic, Uhol, Humenne, Kozma, Russki, Zadan-Arbov, Rometov, Znaeov, Bilovarci, Hrusov, Solm, Hlotkov, and other places as well.[18] Two of the most famous monasteries were those of Saint Michael at Hrusov and Saint Nicholas of Cerneca Hora, "Black Mountain" in Mukachevo.

Saint Michael of Hrusov

The Monastery of Saint Michael existed for some time before the year 1243, for in that year the monks petitioned the Hungarian King Bela IV for a grant to rebuild their library which was destroyed in the Tartar invasion.[19]

In the early sixteenth century, a German named Scheifeld Fiel brought the recently discovered art of printing to Carpatho-Russia by setting up at the monastery of Saint Michael a printing press which published several liturgical books: the *Priest's Prayerbook,* the *Pentecostarion,* and the *Lenten Triodion* among them.[20] This monastery housed the first theological school known in *Karpatska Rus'* and undertook the training of priests. The monastery, however, was sadly burned to the ground about 1657 in the religious wars between the Protestant and Roman Catholic Hungarian nobles.[21]

Saint Nicholas the Wonderworker of Cerneca Hora

The Monastery of Saint Nicholas has its origins in obscurity. Some historians claim that it was in existence before the Hungarians came to *Karpatska Rus'* and was founded in the middle of the eleventh century. Others claim that it was founded through the efforts of Prince Theodore Korjatovich who migrated in 1339 from Galician Russia with a large number of followers. The Hungarian king gave him the province of Mukachevo and it was at the town of Mukachevo itself that prince Theodore founded this monastery that was later to be well-known among Carpatho-Russians. Mukachevo was to be the ecclesistical center for Carpatho-Russia until 1818 when the

7

diocese of Mukachevo was split into the diocese of Mukachevo and the diocese of Presov.

The Creation of the "Uniate" Church

By the second half of the sixteenth century, the Protestant Reformation had reached the territories ruled by the Hungarian princes including Carpatho-Russia. Lutheranism became widespread in Slovakia and Calvinism in Transylvania. The political wars between the princes of Transylvania and those who favored the Hapsburg dynasty became a religious war. The pro-Hapsburgs were Roman Catholic while the Transylvanians were Protestants. Caught in between were the Orthodox Carpatho-Russians, whose lands were divided between the two opposing forces: Prjasevska Rus' (the area about Presov) came under Roman Catholic control while the area around Mukachevo was controlled by the Protestants.[22]

Cut off from the diocesan see at Mukachevo, the Carpatho-Russians in Prjasevska Rus apparently strengthened their old ties with the Orthodox diocese of Peremysl, leading to an increase in Orthodox icons, service books, and other religious articles from Galicia.[23] However, the Orthodox in Galicia, through the instigations of the Jesuit Order, found that the Polish Roman Catholic crown to which they were subject wanted to bring them into the fold of the Roman Church.

The Orthodox of Carpatho-Russia and Galicia, like their brethren in the other Orthodox lands, refused to accept the innovations of the Roman Church and retained their Orthodox faith even after the break between Rome and the Orthodox Patriarch of Constantinople in 1054. Saint Methodios, as early as 880, had to defend not only the Slavonic services he was promulgating but also the Orthodox teaching concerning the procession of the Holy Spirit, as stated in the Nicene-Constantinopolitan Creed, against the Latin bishops.[24]

In the early fifteenth century, the emperor of Constantinople led a delegation of Orthodox bishops, which included the patriarch of Constantinople, to Italy to discuss with the pope the possibility of a reunion between the two Churches. The motivation for this union was not so much spiritual as political. The Byzantine Empire was being quickly gobbled up by the Turks, very little was left outside of the city of Constantinople. It was hoped that if a reunion was achieved the pope would call a crusade to save Constantinople.[25] The theological discussions took place at the Council of Florence in 1439; all but two of the Orthodox signed the document of reunion. When the delegation returned to Constantinople, the reunion was repudiated by the people; Bishop Mark of Ephesos, one who refused to sign the document, was regarded as a saint shortly after his death.

The stillborn agreement of Florence was used by the Roman Catholics as the vehicle to unite the Orthodox of Galicia and White Russia with the Roman Church. The promise of a better social and political status in the framework of the Polish kingdom prompted the union more than any theological or spiritual consideration. In 1596, there was a meeting of several hierarchs from Galicia and White Russia at the town of Brest. A union with the Roman Catholic Church was proclaimed according to the principles of Florence. The former Orthodox, now "united with Rome," were permitted to keep all of their externals of worship, including the liturgical tradition of Constantinople, which they followed, and their discipline which included a married priesthood. But they had to submit to Roman theology and doctrine and to acknowledge the primacy of jurisdiction of the pope of Rome.[26]

While the hierarchy attached themselves to the Roman Church to form a "united" or popularly called "Uniate" Church, the priests and laypeople were furious. As the Council of Brest was taking place, another council met, attended by the representative of the Ecumenical Patriarch of Constantinople, three bishops, two hundred priests, and a large group of lay people. The "Orthodox Council" of Brest deposed those bishops who joined the Roman Church, invoking the authority of the Ecumenical Patriarch who held jurisdiction over the territories involved.[27]

The Polish crown and the Uniate bishops repudiated the "Orthodox Council" and outlawed the Orthodox faith. To be Orthodox was not only to be a second-class citizen and be discriminated against. It now also meant to be an outlaw subject to civil penalties. Despite this the Orthodox people clung to their faith and organized into "Orthodox Brotherhoods" with the support of the Ecumenical Patriarchate of Constantinople, and put up a stiff resistance to the Uniate churches for a long time.[28] In the eighteenth century the Uniates were given the term "Greek Catholic," a term which showed that they were Catholics who followed the Greek[29] rite of the Church of Constantinople rather than Roman Catholics who followed the rite of the Church of Rome.[30]

The Union of Uzhorod

The first attempt to bring the Orthodox Carpatho-Russians into the Uniate Church was the work of Prince Gyorgy Drugeth III (d. 1620). A Protestant who converted to Roman Catholicism, Drugeth believed that the "religion of the ruler is the religion of the land," and with the cooperation of the Uniate bishop of Peremysl and the Roman bishop of Hungarian Eger, he planned to unite the Orthodox Carpatho-Russians of his territories in the area of Hummene with Rome in 1614.[31] His efforts failed because the Orthodox bishop of Mukachevo refused to take part and was supported by the Protestant Transylvanian princes who saw the "Greek Catholic" Church as a further strengthening of the Roman Catholic Hapsburg dynasty.[32]

The second attempt to form a Uniate Church in Carpatho-Russia took place in 1646 at the town of Uzhorod. At that time, sixty-three priests pledged their loyalty to

Rome in the chapel of the fort at Uzhorod. The bishop of neighboring Mukachevo, Basil Tarasovich, had earlier sought to become a Uniate and through the Roman bishop of Eger went to the capital of Vienna to approach the Roman Catholic hierarchy there. In 1642, he formally joined the Uniate Church and requested the Austrian court to install him as the Uniate bishop of Mukachevo. However, George Rakoczy I, the Protestant prince over the Mukachevo area, was strongly opposed to Tarasovich and the Uniate Church. He appointed John Jusko as the Orthodox bishop of Mukachevo and, in fact, Mukachevo had an Orthodox bishop until 1693, long after the Union of Uzhorod.[33]

The Union of Uzhorod was strictly an oral agreement. There is no written record of it. In 1648, the Uniate priests who agreed to the union met and elected Peter Parthens Rostosinsky as their bishop. Peter Parthens appeared with his priests at a synod of Hungarian Roman Catholic clergy which was held in Trnava in Slovakia and asked to be recieved with the priests and consecrated a bishop into the Catholic Church.[34] The Roman Catholic primate of Hungary, George Lippey, reported the union to Rome after some delay perhaps because he did not want a Uniate bishop in Mukachevo.[35] The terms of what has become known as the Union of Uzhorod granted three privileges to the Carpatho-Russian Uniates: they were allowed to keep their ritual and liturgical customs; they were to have equal status with the Roman clergy, socially and politically; and they could elect their own bishop.[36]

When no response from Rome was forthcoming, the Uniate priests took Peter Parthens to Romania and in the guise of being Orthodox themselves had him consecrated bishop by the Orthodox metropolitan of Transylvania.[37] In 1652, Bishop Peter Parthens called a conference of his clergy and prepared a written account of the 1646 Union of Uzhorod, listing the names of the original sixty-three priests who gave an oral agreement. Attached to the document were the signatures of four hundred priests who attended the 1652 meeting. [38] In 1655, Peter Parthens was confirmed as bishop by Rome and given full episcopal authority.[39] The Roman Catholic primate of Hungary, George Lippey, absolved him of the irregularity incurred when he was consecrated by Orthodox bishops and gave him jurisdiction over all Carpatho-Russian Uniates in Hungary. However a Uniate diocese of Mukachevo was not created, and the Uniate bishop became the vicar general of the Roman Catholic bishop of Eger until such a diocese was finally established in 1771.[40]

Orthodoxy continued to exist in Carpatho-Russia until the middle of the eighteenth century.[41] The union was popular with the clergy, since it improved their social and political status. In Hungary the Orthodox priests were serfs; they belonged to the landowner just as did the Orthodox lay people. The Uniate priests were freed from serfdom and given (in theory) an equal place of respect along with their Roman counterparts. They were given material support from the government to bring their poverty to an end. Their children were allowed to be educated. Small wonder that the Uniate movement was a success with many clergymen!

However it was not a success with all and certainly not with all the lay people. Quite frequently it had to be implemented by force and often churches were seized by Roman Catholic priests who had no intention of allowing them to be used by Orthodox or even the "Greek Catholics." Thus Dr. Nicholas Beskid, a Greek Catholic priest himself, writes,

> Accompanied by the police, the civic authorites surrounded the church (Carpatho-Russian Orthodox), broke down the doors and as soon as a Roman Catholic priest placed unleavened bread on the altar, the church with this act was considered to be Roman Catholic. And wherever the people protested against such terrorism they were beaten up, and those who revolted were thrown into jail from which they were not released until

they became Roman Catholics.[42]

The Orthodox faith was outlawed formally and, as late as 1914, ninety-four Carpatho-Russian peasants were given prison terms and stiff fines simply for professing the Orthodox faith at the infamous Marmaros-Sighet trials. Their Orthodoxy was held to be "high treason against the Hungarian state."[43] In similar circumstances, a young Carpatho-Russian Orthodox priest, Fr. Maxim Sandovich, trained in Pochaev in Russia because of the status of Orthodoxy in the Austro-Hungarian Empire, was executed for his profession of the Orthodox faith in 1914.[44]

Despite the fact that the Carpatho-Russian people found themselves in the Uniate "Greek Catholic" Church, they did not forget that they were members of the Orthodox faith. They heard the word *Pravoslavnij*, "Orthodox," still in the services of the Church. The mention of Saint John Chrysostom, patriarch of Constantinople, at the conclusion of the Sunday Divine Liturgy reminded them of their spiritual roots. The union was regarded by many as an empty political device, a jurisdictional recognition of the pope of Rome. If asked if they were Catholics, the average priest or lay person would respond "*Ja ne katolik, Ja Russnak!*"—"I am not a Catholic, I am Russian!"[45]

This response also indicates the degree to which the "Greek Catholic" Church became the bearer of Carpatho-Russian culture and the degree to which it preserved its identity in the face of Hungarian attempts to suppress or destroy it outright. In the period of Turkish rule the Orthodox Church of Greece preserved Greek culture in the same way. It was not unusual to have some Carpatho-Russians claim their nationality as "Greek Catholic," something that is explained by the close relationship of the Greek Catholic Church and Carpatho-Russian culture.

There have always been and still are many "closet Orthodox" in the ranks of the Uniate Church. The Rev. Alexander Duchnovich (1803-1865), called the "national

13

awakener of Carpatho-Russian people," published a "Liturgical Catechism" in 1851, written in Church Slavonic. In this work, although a member of the Greek Catholic Church and supposed to follow Roman doctrine, he attributed the consecration of the bread and wine during the Liturgy not to the words of institution—the teaching of the Roman Church—but to the *epiclesis*—the teaching of the Orthodox Church.[46] In the second edition of the Liturgical Catechism, this chapter was omitted at the request of the Austrian Papal Nuncio because it was Orthodox and not Roman Catholic doctrine.[47]

At the end of his *History of the Eparchy of Prjasev*, Duchnovich remarks: "the Greek Catholic clergy like to preserve the ancient ecclesiastical discipline."[48] Although he made this remark to show that until the Greek Catholic clergy began to study with Latin rite seminarians they had beards like their Orthodox counterparts, this was also true of other more weighty matters of church life as well.

According to the Hungarian historian of the Hapsburg Monarchy of the Austro-Hungarian Empire, Oscar Jaszi, the Pan-Slav movement of the late nineteenth century, which called the Slav peoples to rally around Orthodoxy and the Russian Czar, found support in Carpatho-Russia not only because of financial promises "but also by utilizing the deep religious mysticism of the people, which instinctively resented the Papal union of its clergy, on which the old Orthodox religion had a great sentimental appeal."[49]

The Organization of the Greek Catholic Church in Carpatho-Russia

In 1771, through the influence of Empress Maria Theresa, the diocese of Mukachevo, the traditional see of the Orthodox bishops in Carpatho-Russia, was established by Pope Clement XIV to be the see of the Uniate bishop of Carpatho-Russia. (An Orthodox bishop functioned in Mukachevo until 1690.)[50] Prior to this time, the Uniate

14

bishop functioned, as mentioned above, as a suffragan of the Roman Catholic bishop of Eger. The second bishop of the Uniato dioccsc of Mukachevo, Andrew Bachinsky (1773 to 1809), restructured it totally. Though the name of the diocese remained the same, he transferred the seat from Mukachevo to Uzhorod, and at the same time established a seminary there as well.

In 1818, the Vatican established a second diocese, that of Presov, with its center in the same town. A seminary was established in this diocese in 1880. Before this the clergy of the Presov diocese were trained at either Uzhorod or one of the Roman Catholic seminaries.[51]

The existence of these two dioceses and seminaries was to have an effect on the Greek Catholic Church in America in later years. Since the hometown of Orestes Chornock fell within the bounds of the Presov diocese, it was only natural that he would attend the Presov Seminary and be assigned as a priest in this diocese.

The Spiritual Life of the Greek Catholic Church at the Turn of the Century

The Greek Catholic Church stood at the center of life for the average Carpatho-Russian peasant just as much at the turn of the century as in the previous centuries of its existence. If a peasant was at the bottom of the social ladder in the Hungarian Empire, within the walls of his church he was at the top, outranked only by the saints. The feasts of the Church provided him with rest in his labors, while its fasts reminded him that the Savior Himself lived in poverty and was ill-treated just as he was.

Pilgrimages were popular among the people; they served perhaps as a vacation serves us in society today. One of the most popular places was Maria Poc in Hungary, whose monastery church housed a weeping icon that was revered by the Roman as well as the Greek Catholics. The Monastery of Cerneca Hora of Mukachevo, whose Orthodox monks were replaced by Uniate "Basilian" after the

15

Union was firmly established, was also a popular place where pilgrimage, *Otpust,* took place on the feast of the Dormition of the Birthgiver of God.[52] Another popular place of pilgrimage was the Holy Spirit Monastery at Krasnobrod whose monastery church also contained a miraculous icon of the Birthgiver of God. By far and away the average church-goer, though illiterate, came to love the Christ whose teaching and miracles he eagerly listened to as the Gospel was read each Sunday.

Although the Greek Catholic Church in the Austro-Hungarian Empire was supported by the state, the members of the churches were expected to do their share in the form of the *koblina* and *rokovina,* duties that the peasants owed to the Greek Catholic priest. The *koblina* was payable in agricultural products or currency; the *rokovina* demanded physical labor in the fields of the priest.[53] This system often proved to be a source of conflict between the priests and their people until it was formally abolished in 1920.

Very often the priests, educated in a strong Hungarian environment, came to look down upon their Carpatho-Russian culture and language, which they spoke only condescendingly to their parishoners, preferring to converse in Hungarian among themselves. This was particularly true of the clergy trained at the Uzhorod Seminary. [54] This pro-Hungarian tendency often led to a rift between the clergy and their flocks and also often led to an increased desire to identify with the Roman Catholic Church and to encourage "Latinization" of the Church.

On the other hand, the clergy trained at Presov tended to be more inclined toward Carpatho-Russian culture. Unlike the Uzhorod clergy who liked to pattern themselves after the Hungarian aristocracy, the Presov clergy lived with the people and took an interest in their welfare.[55]

Although there were scattered attempts to return to the Orthodox Church in the 1760s, at the beginning of the twentieth century the village of Iza in Marmaros county, which was one of the places where Orthodoxy survived the longest after the Union of Uzhorod, returned to Orthodoxy in 1903. This return paved the way for a larger return following World War I when Orthodoxy again became legal in 1919 in the post-war Czechoslovak republic.[56]

When Fr. Orestes Chornock became the rector of the parish church in Osturna in 1906, he had no idea of the role he would play in the Greek Catholic Church in America. In Osturna, a town of some two thousand people in the most western part of Carpatho-Russia, life continued on at its slow rural pace. Orthodoxy was a part of a distant memory from ages past and those who returned to it in the Austro-Hungarian Empire were punished as agents of the czar. The newly ordained pastor of Osturna was doubtless more concerned with meeting his parishioners, visiting the sick, celebrating the Sacraments and the cycle of feastdays: in short the things that all pastors are concerned with.

1. His Eminence as a child sitting next to his father, the Rev. John Chornock, with brothers Myron and Emil.

2. As a graduate of the Presov Gymnasium in 1902.

3. As a newly ordained priest in 1906.

4. Pani Yolanda Chornock (Fell asleep in the Lord, †May 28, 1937).

5. The parish in Sariske Jastrebije where Fr. John
Chornock had served as pastor.

Chapter 2

THE PROMISED LAND

At the turn of the century Carpatho-Russians lived in one of the poorest areas of the Austro-Hungarian Empire. The vast majority of them were peasants and worked small plots of land or were day laborers on the farms of others. Eighty percent lived in villages of less than two thousand people. There was little social or geographic mobility; ninety-seven percent of Carpatho-Russians in rural areas, (that is most of the population), married other Carpatho-Russians who were like themselves members of the Greek Catholic Church, and died in the same village in which they were born and lived. [1]

As peasants Carpatho-Russians had a strong attachment to the land. Land ownership was a symbol of success, a sign of status. The lack of land available at home, caused by an increase in population and inefficient farming practices, and at times a fear of being drafted into the

Imperial army, led many young men to leave their native land and emigrate to the United States in the late nineteenth and early twentieth centuries.[2] At this time also the Hungarian government was moving toward adopting a policy that would lead to the assimilation of the Carpatho-Russian people into the Hungarian ethnic mold. All Greek Catholics were considered "Magyars of the Greek Catholic faith" whether they were Carpatho-Russian, Slovak or Hungarian.[3] Carpatho-Russians were encouraged to "Magyarize" their names and, in 1907, a new law directed teachers to encourage "consciousness of membership in the Hungarian nation."[4] The language of instruction in schools became almost exclusively Hungarian and teachers, Greek Catholic priests, and government officials, though most often Carpatho-Russians themselves, fostered the Hungarian ideal to improve their own social and political status. The result of this policy was an identity crisis for the average Carpatho-Russian who often did not have a clear idea of his ethnic origins.

At the turn of the century American industry was booming and needed cheap labor. As early as 1877, Carpatho-Russia and Slovakia were visited by agents from American coal mines who were seeking to recruit the peasants to work as strike breakers.[5] Factories and even shipowners sent agents to enlist these people to work in the New World.

The letters of these first immigrants sent back home encouraged their countrymen to join them in the United States. The Carpatho-Russian peasant, on hearing that the twenty-five to thirty-five cents he earned at the end of a fourteen hour day could be made in America in one hour of work, was only too happy to consider the prospect of immigration.[6] Freedom of speech and religion, the absence of a military draft, freedom from Hungarian political exploitation, all served to make the move almost irresistable.

The Hungarian government, faced with the depopulation of entire areas, attempted to curb this immigration through the use of border patrols and by having the Catholic clergy preach against it; methods that were far from effective. Paying for passage was another problem faced by the Carpatho-Russian who wished to emigrate to America. Land was either sold or the money borrowed from relatives who were in America already or from Jewish money lenders.

Most Carpatho-Russians came to the United States between the years 1899 and 1914 when World War I made the passage almost impossible.[7] They settled largely in the industrial areas of the Northeast, especially in New York, Pennsylvania, New Jersey, and Ohio where they worked in factories and coal mines.

The First Carpatho-Russian Churches

Next to acquiring a house to live in, one of the first things that the new immigrants did was to band together to construct a church. Even more so than in Europe, the church in America became the religious and social center of Carpatho-Russian life. America was a land that could be quite hostile; there was a great deal of prejudice against all Slav immigrants from American society which saw their culture and language as inferior to Anglo-Saxon culture. In addition, since the Slavs frequently worked for lower wages and as strike breakers, the older immigrant groups, particularly the Irish who were being displaced by them, saw the new immigrants as a direct threat to their well-being. The church was a place that offered shelter from all of this hostility and the freedom to converse *po nasemu* ("our way") without the fear of reproach. In short, the church was an island of the old country in the multi-ethnic American sea.

The first churches that the Carpatho-Russians built in the United States were almost all, with one exception, in the coal mining regions of eastern Pennsylvania, the exception being Saint Mary's of Minneapolis, Minnesota. In October of 1890, the ten Greek Catholic priests serving churches in the United States were invited to attend a meeting to discuss common problems at the invitation of Fr. Alexis Toth, the pastor of Saint Mary's of Minneapolis.[8] The meeting was held in Wilkes-Barre, Pennsylvania on October 17, 18, and 19, in the rectory of Fr. Alexlander Dzubay.[9]

The minutes of the meeting reveal the problems that were being faced in the Greek Catholic Church in America at the time. One of the main problems was the raising of funds for and the organization of parishes. This was an important issue simply because in America the churches were usually organized by the people even before a priest was able to serve the parish. According to Roman Canon law, because their was no Greek Catholic bishop in the United States at the time, the people should have sought out the blessing of the local Roman Catholic bishop to build their church. Sometimes this was done, especially since many banks wanted the bishop's signature on any mortgage. More often though, no bishop was consulted and the church was built and incorporated "independently" of the local Roman hierarch. This practice was strictly against the canon law of both the Roman Catholic and Orthodox Churches, although later the practice allowed many former Uniates, who returned to Orthodoxy, to retain their church properties.

Another serious problem was a growing anxiety about the role of the Latin Rite hierarchy in the American Greek Catholic Church. The Greek Catholic priests in the New World, because they had no bishop of their own, were technically under the jurisdiction of the local Roman Catholic ordinaries, most of whom had a dim view of the Greek Catholic Church, if they had any at all. The priests at the conference in Wilkes-Barre resolved to ask their European bishops to give them a representative in the United States and not to abandon them to the Roman bishops who "lack knowledge of our Greek Rite Catholic Church and its agreement in the pact of Union,[10] and thus the Latin Rite bishops and clergy do not feel obligated by them."[11]

The assembled priests also asked that their bishops, in line with the above, send only married men to the United States and to "inform Rome that in our Greek Rite Catholic Church most of the priests are married, and only a few remain celibate. Our faithful accept and highly respect our married clergy, more so than the single clergy."[12]

Other proposals at the conference dealt with the organization of parishes and the regulation of church funds and properties and societies within the church.[13] The fathers assembled also established, at the motion of Fr. Theophan Obruskevic, a newspaper naming it *Novyj Svit (New World)*.[14]

The concerns of the conference of Greek Catholic priests about being forced into the Roman Catholic Church were not imaginary. The Roman Catholic bishops and clergy were for the most part ignorant of the "Greek Rite" Church and were not at all sympathetic to its existence in the United States, especially at a time when the American Catholic Church was beginning to emerge as a consolidated organization with a stress on its American identity.

For example, the January 1915 issue of the *Ecclesiastical Review,* a publication intended for American Roman Catholic clergy, contained an article entitled "Some Thoughts on the Ruthenian Question" which illustrates the wall of ignorance and prejudice that the early Greek Catholic faithful and clergy were confronted with in facing the American Roman Catholic Church:

"Compared with the Latin Rite, the Byzantine is and always will be in a state of inferiority. The Latin is universal, since it compromises many nationalities, none of which can claim the language of the sacred ceremonies as its own . . . . Nowadays when people try to compile an Esperanto language that shall serve to unite all the peoples into one common fellowship for trade and business purposes, the Catholic of the Latin Rite may proudly point to his Church, which has never given up the common bond of unity, but has kept steadfastly to the old language. This is just the thing the Byzantine rite has not done. This rite . . . has been everywhere translated into the language of its followers. Instead of being the vehicle of unity, it has often become the very agent of strife and disunion."[15]

The article continues:

It is not necessary to discuss here whether it is an advantage, political or otherwise, that such a "national" church (i.e. "Ruthenian") should exist in Europe. Certainly it has no raison d'être in America. The government of Canada or of the United States is under no fear that a Slav state will spring up in the New World. Why then should there be a Slavonic Church? Probably the Ruthenians who emigrate to Canada and the United States will remain Ruthenians for some years, but their descendants born there will speak no other language but English. They will not feel at home in a church that by its very name presents itself as un-American. The economy of the Catholic Church is not like that of national churches. She tolerates national sections in the Old World for the sake of peace. But there appears no reason for keeping up these divisions artifically in the new world. The Germans or Poles or Italians who settle in America do not set up a German or Polish or Italian church. Hence, the Ruthenians cannot have any logical claim to the distinction, unless it be for a time only to favor gradual naturalization.

The author continues to point out that,

23

The old-Salvonic language in the Liturgy is a strange growth to the ears of English speaking people whose religious vocabulary shows the clear signs of its Latin origin. The outcome of all this is that they (the descendants of the immigrants) will wish to become Latins . . ." The Church protects the national rite in its own home, but she has no reason for keeping it up artificially amid surroundings to which it foreign.[16]

To be sure there were some who sought fair treatment for the Greek Catholic Church in America, but their voices were not heard by the American hierarchy nor for that matter by the Vatican. The American Roman Catholic bishops and the Vatican both failed to take into account the total identification of the Carpatho-Russian and Galician peasants with the life of their church—not the Roman Church but their own Greek Catholic Church.

In fact, what the author of the article in the *Ecclesiastical Review* just quoted failed to realize, what the American Catholic hierarchy failed to realize, and what the Vatican itself failed to realize was what was perceived in Roman circles as the greatest weakness of the "Byzantine Rite"—the fact that everywhere it went it became "enculturated"—was at the same time its greatest strength, enabling it to survive both "Turkokratia" and modern day Communist oppression. Had the Roman Catholic Church been able to appreciate this unique identification of church and culture, the story of the Greek Catholic Church in America would have been written differently. As it was though, articles such as the above served only to confirm the fears of the Greek Catholic clergy and faithful that they were "second class members" of the Roman Catholic Church whose spiritual inheritance was worthless and whose continued existence as Greek Catholics was seriously being called into question in the New World.

24

Fr. Toth—the First Return to Orthodoxy

One of the initiators of the October 1890 Greek Catholic Clergy Conference was Fr. Alexis Toth, the pastor of Saint Mary's Greek Catholic Church of Minneapolis, Minnesota. Fr. Toth was a widower and the former professor of canon law at the Presov Seminary. He had been given leave to go to America to both serve the parish in Minneapolis and to report to Bishop John Valyj of the Presov diocese on the spiritual condition of the Greek Catholics in America.[17] At the advice of Bishop Valyj and in accordance with the principles of Canon Law of the Roman Church, he presented himself to Archbishop John Ireland, in whose jurisdiction the Minneapolis church fell, on December 19, 1890, two months after the October Wilkes-Barre meeting. Here is his account of the meeting:

I arrived in America as a Uniate, as a former professor of church law. I was fully aware that in America I, as a Uniate, must obey the Latin Rite bishop in whose diocese I will serve. This is demanded by the Union (of Uzhorod) and several papal decrees, because there is no Greek Rite Catholic bishop in the United States of America. All this was written in my credentials. The city of my appointment was Minneapolis, Minnesota, in the archdiocese of Archbishop John Ireland.

As a faithful Uniate and acting on the advice of Bishop John Valyj, I presented myself to Archbishop John Ireland on December 19, 1890, kissing his hand (without a genuflection—that was my great mistake which I later recognized). I handed my accreditations to the archbishop. I well remember that just as he had read that I was a Greek Rite Catholic, his hands began to tremble . . . It took the archbishop about fifteen minutes to read my accreditations, after he firmly questioned me (the conversation was in Latin). "Do you have a wife?" I replied, "No, but I had one, I am a

25

widower." When the archbishop heard this he threw my documents on the table and in a loud voice shouted: " I have already sent a protest to Rome not to send such priests here." I asked the Archbishop, "What kind of priests do you mean?" The Archbishop's reply was, "Such as you are." I replied, "After all, I am a Catholic priest of the Greek Rite, I am a Uniate and was validly ordained by a Catholic bishop." The archbishop, "I do not consider you, nor your bishop, a Catholic. Furthermore, there is not need here for a Greek Rite Catholic priest. We have a Polish priest; he can be the priest for the Greek Rite Catholics." I replied, "But he is of the Latin Rite; our people will not understand him nor turn to him . . . they even built a church for themselves." Archbishop Ireland replied, "I did not give them permission, neither will I give you jurisdiction to work here." I was bitter over such rude fanaticism from a representative of the papal church, so I sharply replied, "In such case I do not need your jurisdiction nor your absolution. I know the laws of the Catholic Church. I know how the union was established and in such manner I will go forward . . ." The archbishop became pale white and so did I. Word after word followed, so that it was not worthwhile to renew the conversation.[18]

Despite the prohibitions of Archbishop Ireland, Fr. Toth continued his work in Minneapolis and wrote to the Greek Catholic bishop of Presov concerning the manner in which Archbishop Ireland received him. After the third such letter he received a response from Canon Joseph Dzubay cautioning patience. He was also instructed to write down an account of what happened at his meeting with Ireland, which was to have been sent to Rome.[19] However, the Greek Catholic authorities were reluctant to forward Fr. Toth's account to the Vatican, possibly because they were afraid of excaberating an already bad situation or, more likely they simply did not want to become involved in a controversy that was thousands of miles away which could ultimately affect their own status in the Roman Catholic Church.

Although Bishop Ireland tried to seize control of the Minneapolis church through a legal suit and thus stop the activities of Fr. Toth, the lawsuit was won by Saint Mary's and Fr. Toth. These actions only convinced Fr. Toth to do what he had been thinking of doing for a long time—return to the Orthodox Church of his ancestors.

> I made up my mind (he later related), to do something which I carried in my heart for a long time, for which my soul longed, that is to become Orthodox. But how was it to be done? I had to be very cautious. The unfortunate Union, the source of our decline and all our ills, had been part of our people for too long. We had already borne that yoke on our shoulders for 250 years. I fervently prayed to God to grant me the power to make all this clear to my unenlightened parishoners.[20]

On March 25, 1891, the Sunday of Orthodoxy, Bishop Vladimir of San Francisco, Fr. Toth and the 365 members of Saint Mary's Church in Minneapolis, were accepted into the Russian Orthodox diocese of Alaska and the Aleutian Islands.[21] Through Fr. Toth the spark of Orthodoxy was fanned into flame once again in the hearts of Carpatho-Russians. Fr. Toth soon left Minneapolis and went to Wilkes-Barre, Pennsylvania, the heart of the Carpatho-Russian immigration, where he continued to spread the Orthodox faith among Carpatho-Russian Uniates.

Fr. Toth was bitterly attacked in the Uniate press, being compared with Judas Iscariot and with the archheretic Arius,[22] and Orthodoxy was branded as the "faith of Toth." The second conference of Greek Catholic Clergy meeting in Hazelton, Pennsylvania, condemned the action

27

of Fr. Toth, even though they all protested the ongoing Latin Rite oppression of their church and threatened to refuse to obey the Holy See if their demands were not met and their rite was not protected.[23] The local newspaper, *The Daily Speaker* of Hazelton of December 3/4 1891, reported it was at this meeting that the "Greek Catholic Union" (Greko-Katholiceskoje Sojedinenije) was founded. The newspaper also reported that if the communication that was sent to the Pope was not favorably received, the priests would elect one of their own number as bishop and proceed independently with the work of the Greek Catholic Church in America.[24]

This outlines what the Greek Catholic Clergy in America felt was one of their strongest needs, the need to have their own bishop and separate ecclesiastical organization in America, apart from the Roman Catholic Church.

Internal Dissensions

Fr. Toth's Orthodoxy missionary activities and the hostility of the Roman Catholic hierarchy were compounded in the late 1890s and the early 1900s by internal division among the Uniate clergy themselves. The priests who came from Galicia began to identify themselves with the nascent "Ukrainian" movement that was being fostered in the "old country" by the Austrian government for political purposes. These clergy often became extreme nationalists and eventually succeeded in creating a "Ukrainian" Catholic Church in America with its own bishop in 1924, separate from the rest of the "Ruthenians."

Another internal division existed among the clergy who rejected the "Ukrainianism" found among the Galician immigrants. The source of the conflict was to be found in the seminary backgrounds of the priests, whether they had attended the seminary at Uzhorod or the seminary at Presov. The priests from the Uzhorod Seminary tended to follow the ways of the old Hungarian government and of the Roman Catholic Church, and tended to have an "elitist" spirit in their relationship with their parishioners. From a purely social point of view the city of Uzhorod was located inside a predominantly Hungarian region and there was a tendency among the Slavs living there—clergy included—to assimilate the Hungarian culture.

On the other hand, the city of Presov was located well within a predominantly Slavic area, and the clergy of the Presov Seminary identified with Slav culture and language in general and often with Great Russian culture in particular. Writing about the turmoil over national identity that existed in *Karpatska Rus* following the break-up of the old Austro-Hungarian Empire, Dr. Paul Magosci writes:

> In the Presov region, only these two orientations existed: the Russian or Russophile, and the local Rusyn, although it was often difficult to distinguish between the two. Both claimed that they were Carpatho-Russian (*karpato-russkij*), that they were maintaining the tradition of nineteenth-century national leaders like Duchnovich, Dobranskyj, Sabov and Silvaj, and that they were opposed to the introduction of the artificial Ukrainian jargon from Galicia which was being used in Sub-Carpathian Rus.[25]

As a result of their location, the Presov clergy identified with Slavic culture in general and emphasized their "Carpatho-Russian" roots. Though they also were required to know the "official" Hungarian language, the Presov clergy lived "with their flocks," so to speak, and placed a strong emphasis on the "separateness" of their "Eastern Rite" Church and the privileges of the Union of Uzhorod. From time to time some of their number would flirt with "Great Russian" language and culture and even Orthodoxy. It comes as no surprise then that Fr. Alexis Toth, the former director of the Presov Seminary, who also served it as professor of canon law and church history, brought with him from his seminary experience the "seeds" of his return to Orthodoxy in America. He wrote to his bishop in 1896, several years after his return to the Orthodox faith: "Without any ulterior motives I united with Orthodoxy about which I already dreamed in the Old Country."[26] In speaking of these two seminaries we must also point out that there were many individual exceptions to these general remarks. Not everyone from the Presov school shared the sentiments of Fr. Duchnovich or Fr. Toth's dreams of Orthodoxy, some like the "Apostolic Visitator Hodobay" were in fact strongly "pro-Hungarian." Nor were all of the Uzhorod clergy "pro-Hungarian" or "pro-Latin." But these general tendencies did exist and in America the clergy frequently designated themselves as "Presov" or "Uzhorod."

Far from being a simple rivalry between two schools, the often subtle, often open, conflict between the Presov clergy and their "Carpatho-Russian" orientation and the Uzhorod clergy with their "Hungarian" orientation was a reflection of the identify crisis that marked the Greek Catholic Church in both the Old Country and America on the spiritual, psychological and social levels.

The Ukrainian and the Presov/Uzhorod conflicts were reflected in the first attempts to give stability to the Greek Catholic Church in America.

The Apostolic Visitator

In November of 1895, Pope Leo XIII issued an encyclical, "Orientaliem Dignitas," which declared that Eastern Rite Catholics should become members of the Roman (Latin Rite) Catholic Church whenever there was no Eastern Rite church to attend. The Orthodox used this decree to show that the Pope was attempting to circumvent the privileges of the Greek Catholics in America. This decree along with an earlier one in 1890, which ordered all Greek Catholic priests who came to America be celibate and be under the authority of the Roman Catholic bishops there, caused several priests and many parishes to return to the Orthodox faith.

In the face of the threat presented by the Orthodox churches as an alternative to remaining Uniate, the open hostilities of the Latin Rite Roman Catholic bishops, and the internal chaos of the Uniate Church in America, the Uniate clergy appealed to the Austro-Hungarian government to come to the aid of the Greek Catholic Church in America. In a pamphlet of 1898, addressed to the Austro-Hungarian government, the Greek Catholic clergy presented the danger of Orthodoxy and the problems and unfair treatment given them by the Roman Catholic bishops. Invoking the memory of Maria Theresa, the Empress who protected the Greek Catholic Church of the Austro-Hungarian Empire in past centuries, the priests requested "leaders of our rite, be independent and fully empowered" so that "we will not be destroyed in faith, rite or nationality."[27]

The Hungarian government was especially interested in stemming the tide of conversions to Orthodoxy. The activities of Fr. Toth had not gone unnoticed in "the old country" and a pamphlet written by him was in circulation there. At this time Orthodoxy was seen as a link with Czarist Russia and, since the czar was the protector of Orthodoxy, the Hungarian government feared that a community of Carpatho-Russian Orthodox in its borders might offer the czar an excuse to "intervene" in their behalf, that is, "armed intervention" and annexation of Hungarian territory.

Though it took time, the pamphlet to the Austro-Hungarian government appeared to have its desired effect. In 1902, at the request of the Hungarian government, the Vatican appointed the Rt. Rev. Andrew Hodobay as the "Apostolic Visitator" for all the "Ruthenians" living in the United States. His task was to make an assessment of the Greek Catholic Church in the United States and to investigate the feasibility of granting it its own bishop.

Initially, the "Fr. Visitator" was given a warm reception by the clergy and faithful, but this initial grace period gave way to a series of bitter attacks in which Hodobay was accused of everything by just about everybody. His credentials were questioned, the Ukrainian faction accused him of being a Hungarian spy, the Uzhorod clergy were opposed to him because he was from Presov, the Presov clergy generally supported him for the same reason, though his "high Hungarian" mannerisms were distasteful to the Presov clergy and the laity. In his dealings with laypeople he perhaps fared the worst. The lay people in the European church had no voice in the affairs of the church per se, but the situation in America was different. The churches in America were organized and financed by the lay people themselves, who often took mortgages against their homes to provide for the construction of the church buildings. The churches were not deeded in trust to the bishop, according to both Roman Catholic and Orthodox canon law but were often chartered by Protestant lawyers as "non-profit corporations." In addition, the initial shortage of Greek Catholic priests in America often caused lay people to assume, in addition to the material responsibilities of the parish, responsibility for its spiritual administration as well. Many of the people also harbored an anti-clerical attitude from the privileged status of the clergy in the peasant economy of the old country. The clergy also were opposed to "Americanization" of the Greek Catholic Church. Few bothered to learn the English language or even to become citizens of the United States preferring the "Old Country" way of life and mannerisms. This was especially true of the Hungarian oriented clergy from Uzhorod.

The chief "opinion maker" of the Greek Catholic community in America from the 1890s to the late 1940s was the "Greek Catholic Union" founded at the second conference of Greek Catholic clergy in 1891 at Hazelton, Pennsylvania, as a fraternal insurance organization. From its inception, the G C U through its newpaper, the *Amerikan-*

skij Russkij Viestnik" (*Russian American Messenger*), took up the fight of the Uniates against both Latinization and Orthodoxy. On the other hand, the lack of a bishop in America left the clergy to be largely "free agents" who often vied against each other for the best parishes and often undermined each other in the eyes of the lay people and the *Amerikanskij Russkij Viestnik*, putting their own welfare ahead of the Church.

Many concerned priests and lay people sought to provide solutions to the lack of organization in the American Greek Catholic Church. A clergy attempt made through the organization of "Saints Cyril and Methodios Society" sought to regulate in 1899 clerical assignments and other related matters through a council of priests. And in 1901, the laity with the aid of the clergy met to organize an "Association of Church Congregations in the United States and Canada."[28] A convention of the organization in 1902 left the Uniate Church more divided than ever. A radical wing wanted a complete break with the Roman Catholic Church and the creation of an "independent" Greek Catholic Church that would be neither Orthodox nor Roman Catholic but organized along the lines of the Episcopal Church.[29] The convention did come to agreement on the right of Uniate churches to be incorporated under the name of the trustee members rather than the bishop, an irregular practice in both the Orthodox and Roman Catholic Churches but familiar in Protestant circles. It also approved a request for a bishop for the Uniate Church in America and the calling for another convention in 1905.[30] The Apostolic Delegate forbade the 1905 "congress" to meet, though some preparation work had been done for it.[31]

Needless to say, the attempts of the "Saints Cyril and Methodios Society" and the "Association of Church Congregations" accomplished little except to point out the pressing need of the American Uniate Church for a bishop of its own.

After having been villified in the Carpatho-Russian newspapers and horribly treated by his own clergy and people, the Rt. Rev. Andrew Hodobay was recalled in 1906. He made a strong recommendation that a bishop be appointed for the Greek Catholics of the United States. The ARV described the work of Hodobay as "a comedy which was played in the United States of America for the last five years" and "this comedy cost the Hungarian government 500,000 kronens."[32] The article further described Hodobay as a Hungarian "secret agent" who lived like "a Turkish Pasha."[33] Hodobay's tendency to be pro-Hungarian gave strength to these charges against him. His use of the Hungarian language in all official correspondence and his great interest in expanding the number of Hungarian Greek Catholic churches, presumably at the expense of the Carpatho-Russian and Galician ones, did nothing to alleviate these suspicions.

In 1907 the Vatican, at the prompting of the Uniate metropolitan of Lvov, Andrew Sheptitsky, consecrated a Basilian monk named Soter Stephen Ortinsky to be the first "Ruthenian" Greek Catholic bishop in the United States. Bishop Ortinsky was a well educated man and an eloquent speaker. He was a Galician by birth and taught in the Basilian seminaries where he was noted for his preaching. But before he even arrived in the United States, Ortinsky was being attacked on two counts: first, that he was a Galician and a supporter of the "Ukrainian" movement; second, that he was not a full bishop, that is, he was only a vicar general who could ordain candidates to the priesthood, but in all ecclesiastical affairs was completely dependent on the local Roman Catholic bishops where his churches were located, even having to secure permission to visit his churches from them beforehand.

When Ortinsky arrived in America he brought with him a new papal bulla entitled *Ea Semper* which of course he was charged to enforce. The *Ea Semper* decree contained the following provisions:

It forbade married men to be ordained to the priesthood in America, and only allowed widowed or celibate priests to work in America.

Uniate priests were forbidden to administer the sacrament of Holy Chrismation, a clear violation of the Eastern tradition.

All candidates for the priesthood would be incardated into the various Latin dioceses.

The Uniate bishop was under the jurisdiction of the Latin Rite bishop wherever he happened to be visiting and could not visit his churches except with the approval of the Latin Rite bishop whose territories they were located in.

The Uniate Bishop could not ordain clerics without the consent of the local Latin Rite Bishop. Other provisions made it easier for the faithful to become Latin Rite Catholics in the cases of mixed marriages and baptisms.

In 1908, the ARV began its attack on the new bishop; at first it directed its protest against the papal decree, later on the competence of the bishop himself. The catalyst for these attacks was the failure of Bishop Ortinsky to give the editor of the ARV, Paul Zatkovich, an audience, on the advice of two clerical advisors. When Bishop Ortinsky sought to change the articles of incorporation of the parishes from lay control to the bishop, according to canon law, the ARV began a campaign against him on this pretext.

The clerical and lay opposition to Ortinsky met in Johnstown on January 12, 1910, and petitioned Rome to recall the bishop. The priests met at Scranton again on August 30, 1911, and sought to organize against the bishop.[34] Ortinsky responded by suspending a total of forty-eight priests who were actively opposed to him.[35] The clergy who supported Ortinsky were labeled traitors and Ukraphils by the ARV.

In 1913, however, Rome granted full jurisdiction to Ortinsky and also further concessions were granted in 1914 with regards to the privisions of *Ea Semper*. Those who opposed the bishop on the grounds that he did not have full jurisdiction were now left without a cause. Ortinsky readmitted the priests who had opposed him after they pledged their obedience. To appease the "Carpatho-Russian" clergy, the chancellor and vicar general of the diocese were appointed from their ranks. Criticisms continued, but for the most part Ortinsky had come out on top. It was a hollow victory though. It has been estimated that the *Ea Semper* decree in fighting that marked most of Ortinsky's episcopacy resulted in the loss of over 90,000 Uniates to the Orthodox Church along with many clergy. Ortinsky did bring some semblance of order to the Greek Catholic Church in America and more than doubled the number of clergy, and consecrated many new churches.[36] The Carpatho-Russian "Rusin" and Ukrainian factions of the church though continued to drift apart. Bishop Ortinsky died of pneumonia on March 24, 1916 in the prime of his life.[37]

Upon the death of Bishop Ortinsky, the Greek Catholic Church was to be jointly governed by Fr. Peter Poniatyshyn and Fr. Gabriel Martyak. In 1918, the Vatican divided the Uniate Church along national lines into a Ukrainian and "Ruthenian" diocese.[38] Frs. Poniatyshyn and Martyak were appointed as administrators of each diocese respectively, and functioned as vicar generals to the local Latin bishops.[39] Of course neither had any episcopal authority.

The period of Fr. Martyak's administration was generally a time of peace and rebuilding. The events of the World War I and the worldwide flu outbreak of the 1920s seemed to take precedence over the affairs of the Greek Catholic Church. Even during this time the clergy and people looked forward to the day when they would have their own Carpatho-Russian bishop, whose presence would bring both peace and order to their Church.

6. Fr. Alexis S. Toth as Orthodox Protopresbyter.

7. October 1890 meeting of Greek Catholic priests, Wilkes-Barre, Pa.

8. Fr. Toth blessing Paschal foods at St. Mary's Church, Minneapolis, Minn.

9. Bishop Orestes Chornock.

Chapter 3

TO THE LAND I WILL SHOW YOU

In the fall of 1908, the congregation of Saint Michael's Greek Catholic Church in the village of Osturna, Spis County, Hungary heard their pastor, Fr. Orestes Chornock, preach his last sermon and bid them farewell. Like so many of their relatives and friends, their pastor of only two years was leaving for America. The Greek Catholics in America needed priests, and Fr. Orestes received the permission of the bishop to immigrate.

The decision of Fr. Orestes to leave Osturna and to come to America was undoubtedly precipitated by the fact that his father-in-law, the Rev. Vladimir Molchany, was one of the pioneer Greek Catholic priests in the United States actively involved in the affairs of the Greek Catholic Church in the late 1890s. He was one of the signatories of the 1898 petition to the Hungarian government to provide the Greek Catholic Church in America with a bishop, as was his brother Rev. Nicholas Molchany. Fr. Vladimir Molchany's parish at the time was Kingston, Pennsylvania.

The early part of the twentieth century was also one of the worst times ever in the history of *Karpatska Rus*. The Hungarian government was pushing hard for the assimilation of its Slavic peoples into the Hungarian fold and the extreme poverty caused almost whole villages to be deserted: their inhabitants in search of a better life in America. With the conditions existing in the Austro-Hungarian Empire and with the reports of his father-in-law in America, it probably did not take Fr. Orestes too long to decide that the future of the Greek Catholic Church and the Carpatho-Russian people lay, not in the "old country," but in the distant land of America.

On November 17, 1908, Fr. Orestes arrived in the United States of America. Bishop Soter Ortinsky assigned him as the pastor of churches in Burnside-Chicago, Illinois for three months, for six months in Cleveland, Ohio and for two years in Dusquene, Pennsylvania. He was described in these years as a pastor "after the heart of Christ," one who worked to fulfill the ideals of the priesthood and served the "Russian people."

Though in later years Fr. Orestes would be described by his enemies as someone who was opposed to legitimate ecclesiastical authority, his activities in the church under Bishop Ortinsky show otherwise. In fact, Fr. Orestes was one of the few Carpatho-Russian priests to stand with Ortinsky, despite the majority who openly attacked him and appealed for his removal. It is interesting to note that many of the priests who would later accuse Fr. Orestes of insubordination to proper authority, at an earlier time had themselves attacked their own Bishop Ortinsky, refusing to submit to his episcopal authority! In one case, a priest, surveying the history of the Greek Catholic Diocese in the United States in the 1940s, accused Fr. Orestes and other of "stubborn refusal to submit to ecclesiastical discipline" not bothering to note that his father was suspended by Bishop Ortinsky for the very same reason, stating that we have reason to believe that "most of the leaders of this movement were moved by a sincere desire to do right . . ."

Fr. Orestes was chosen to be the secretary of a "Mission Circle" formed by the Greek Catholic clergy of the Pittsburgh area on May 18, 1910. The "Mission Circle" was to meet monthly to discuss church and national affairs (i.e. "Carpatho Russian" national affairs). The function of the group was to: 1) Publicly announce loyalty to the bishop; 2) keep the faithful in their ancestral faith — the Greek Catholic Church; 3) work for the repeal of the *Ea Semper* Bulla — something that Ortinsky himself desired 4) enlighten the faithful, leading them in truth; establishing the name "Rusin" as the name of "our Heritage" and establish the newspaper "Rusin" to foster these aims.[1]

Fr. Orestes' steadfast support of Bishop Ortinksy, whom he later remembered as "a good man," as well as his effective pastoral work insured that despite his age (he was only a priest for five years), he would be given even greater responsibilites. On March 25, 1911, he became the pastor of Saint John the Baptist Greek Catholic Church on Arctic Street, Bridgeport, Connecticut, one of the largest, if not the largest Greek Catholic churches in the United States. For the rest of his life Fr. Orestes would never take up permanent residence in any place else. His life would be forever intertwined with the parish of Saint John the Baptist. It was to prove a bitter-sweet relationship.

In the year 1914, Fr. Orestes was appointed dean of his deanery, a position to which Fr. Martyak, as diocesan administrator, re-appointed him as did Bishop Takach in 1925. Saint John's parish was still growing and the demands placed on its pastor are reflected in its metrical records during the first two decades of his pastorate. Typical are the statistics for the year 1917: 216 Baptisms, 42 Weddings, and 48 Funerals.

As a priest Fr. Orestes was zealous not only in the performance of his very demanding pastoral responsibilities, but also in the spiritual life. He insisted on hearing hundreds of confessions, often spending days and nights with penitents. He advocated frequent reception of the sacraments of Confession and Holy Eucharist at a time when a formal, once-a-year reception was the norm.[2]

In addition, Fr. Orestes Chornock possessed a great knowledge of the Byzantine ritual and of Carpatho-Russian ecclesiastical chant, the "prostopinije," a knowledge gained not from reading scholarly studies and journals, but from actual spiritual experience, that is, from *praying* not only the Divine Liturgy but also the Vespers and Matins which he celebrated each feast day, and from reading the "Hours" as often as time permitted. At a time when the Lenten "Presanctified Liturgy" had fallen out of popular use, even among the Orthodox in this country, he faithfully celebrated it on Wednesdays and Fridays of Lent. Under his charismatic direction the parish on Arctic Street became one of the most successful not only in terms of numbers of parishioners and material wealth, but more importantly in spiritual growth. The parishioners found their pastor always ready to receive them, listen to their problems, and to help in any way he could. He frequently provided not only spiritual counsel but material aid from his own resources to those who were in need. One parishioner remembered how Fr. Orestes came with a church officer to his home to collect for the church as was the custom at the time. Seeing that the family was in want, he refused to take anything. However, the parishioner, a small boy at the time, remembers his mother insisted on giving something. Fr. Orestes at last relented and accepted one dollar which he promptly gave to the boy's younger sister "to buy candy with."

Others remember how in the early years of World War II, during the days of food rationing, they were contemplating a "meatless" Easter, a continuation of Great Lent. On Holy Wednesday, late in the evening, they answered a knock at the door to find their beloved pastor with a small gift of ham and kolbassi for them to "make Easter a little bit better." The gifts were arranged by the pastor's friends in New York.

Not having any natural children, though they did have an adopted son, Frances, Fr. Orestes and Pani Yolanda spent their affections on the children of their parish. Fr. Orestes both as a priest and as a bishop frequently remarked that the treasure of any parish was its children; a parish which had few was poor indeed, no matter how much else it had. Fr. Orestes was involved in teaching the children of the parish himself at a time when many pastors were content to leave this responsibility to their cantors.[3]

One of the keys to Fr. Orestes' success in his pastorate was the fact that he was a practical man and adapted himself to the situation of the church in America. At a time when many Greek Catholic rectories had "footbells" to summon the maid, and many priests and panis were concerned with preserving the aristocratic Hungarian life style they had known in Europe, Fr. Orestes was learning to drive an automobile to serve better his parish and was, in fact, one of the first Greek Catholic priests in America to own one. In 1931, he bought a Model "A" Ford and was still driving the "filvver," as he called it, around Bridgeport thirty years later. Fr. Orestes lived with his people, not above them.

Under the leadership of Fr. Orestes, Saint John the Baptist Greek Catholic Church on Arctic Street in Bridgeport became one of the largest and best organized Greek Catholic churches in America during the 1920s. Fr. Orestes himself became well-known as a charismatic and hard-working priest who was concerned not only for his parishioners but for the welfare of the Greek Catholic Church as a whole in the United States.

The Greek Catholic Church in the United States entered the 1920s under the leadership of Fr. Gabriel Martyak for the "Ruthenians," as Rome called the Carpatho-Russians, and Fr. Peter Poniatyshyn for the "Ukrainians." The death of Bishop Ortinsky left the Greek Catholic faithful open to depredations from the Latin Rite clergy, who were always inducing Greek Catholics to join the Roman churches, though this was against Roman canon law. There was also the danger of Greek Catholics leaving the Catholic Church to become Orthodox. This threat loomed large with the consecration of Bishop Alexander Dzubay, a former Greek Catholic priest, as an Orthodox bishop by the Russian Orthodox American Mission for the Carpatho-Russians. He was supposed to head a "Carpatho-Russian Orthodox diocese of Pittsburgh." We shall return to Bishop Dzubay's role in the Carpatho-Russian Churches in America, but suffice to say the turbulence that marked the episcopate of Ortinsky as well as the promise of an Orthodox church with a bishop "of their own blood," induced many to return to the Orthodox faith from the Unia.

The Greek Catholic Union began to work for the appointment of another bishop. The newspaper of the Greek Catholic Union, the *Amerikanskij Russkij Viestnik,* had always served as an "unofficially official" organ of the church in which even Fr. Martyak's administrative appointments and parish assignments were promulgated.

The contacts of the clergy and officers of the Greek Catholic Union were noted by officials in the Vatican and by Bishop Papp of the diocese of Uzhorod in the old country. In March of 1924, two bishops were appointed for the Greek Catholic Church in America: Constantine Bohachevsky, who was to be bishop for the Ukrainians, and Basil Takach, who was to be the bishop for the "Ruthenians," as Rome called the Carpatho-Russians. The Uniate Church in American was now officially split between the two groups.

The split which came about after the death of Ortinsky was now official and was a source of resentment for some of the Carpatho-Russians. There had been an agreement that since Ortinsky was "Ukrainian," his successor would be Carpatho-Russian. The fact that the Ukrainians received their own bishop was felt by some to be unfair. There were also some who wished that Fr. Martyak, the administrator for the Carpatho-Russians, would be selected for the post of bishop, since he was already experienced in the affairs of the Greek Catholic Church. But these potential difficulties were dissolved by the joy that the Greek Catholic Church in America once again had its own bishop, a bishop who would look after its interests and order its affairs.

Bishop Basil Takach was a priest for over twenty years when he was consecrated in Rome together with Bishop Constantine Bohachevsky. Following the example of his uncle, Canon Nicholas Dolinay, who exercised considerable influence over him after his father died when he was only eleven, he elected to remain a celibate priest even though his father was a married priest. Fr. Basil Takach had been a parish priest for eight years, the remainder having been spent at various teaching and administrative posts in the diocesan see of Uzhorod. At the time of his episcopal appointment, he was the spiritual director of the Uzhorod Seminary. He was well-liked by those who knew him and was wished well on his appointment. More importantly, perhaps, was the fact that he had the approval of the new Czechoslovak government. In fact, he was the only church official who welcomed the new Czech authorities in 1918.[4] The others, including his bishop, fled to Hungary rather than recognize a non-Hungarian government.[5] For his loyalty the Czech officials recommended Fr. Basil Takach for the episcopal post in America, undoubtedly with the hope as well that the new bishop would further the cause of Czechoslovakia among the Carpatho-Russian communities in America.

Bishop Takach was consecrated in Rome on June 15, 1924, together with Bishop Bohachevsky and both took possession of their sees on September 1, 1924. Bishop Takach was given a great welcome and during his first pastoral visits was well received.

While the first five years of Bishop Bohachevsky's episcopacy among the Ukrainian Greek Catholics were marked with turmoil, which resulted in the establishment of a Ukrainian Orthodox Church under the Ecumenical Patriarchate of Constantinople[5], Bishop Takach's first five years were marked by a calm that belied the storm brewing beneath it.

In his letter of appointment, his place of residence was given at New York City, but Bishop Takach found it more expedient to move his see from New York to the Pittsburgh area, closer to the majority of the Carpatho-Russian population. He first took up residence in Uniontown, Pennsylvania, and in March of 1926, moved to Homestead, Pennsylvania, where the episcopal residence was established.

Bishop Takach found the Uniate Church in America far different from the Uniate Church in Europe. For one thing, the churches were loosely organized, forming more a confederacy than a solid knit diocese. This was the result of a lack of episcopal authority in the church, especially since there had been no bishop for the last eight years. Contributing to this problem was the fact that most of the parishes were physically owned by the local trustees and the properties had not been incorporated into the diocese under the aegis of the bishop. This situation was fostered by the conditions of life in America; in Europe the government and the wealthy patronized the church and paid the salaries of the clergy. In America the local congregation had to take upon themselves that responsibility. This practice was against the regulations of the Baltimore Synod for the American Catholic Church. Often the hostility of the Roman Catholics caused the fear that if the Roman bishop was deeded the property, he would send a Roman priest. The clergy themselves arranged their transfers often independently of the administrator and even of Bishop Takach, contributing to the lack of structure in the church. The Roman clergy were still, with few exceptions, hostile and whenever they could they induced "Greek Catholics" to become Roman Catholics, though this was strictly against the principles of the Catholic Church.

In dealing with his priests Bishop Takach found that unlike the diocese of Mukachevo, with its seat in Uzhorod, he had to deal with clergy from the Presov diocese as well as those from his own, plus a number of American-born Greek Catholic priests though these were for the most part European-educated. Another problem was the role of the lay people in the Church, especially through the Greek Catholic Union and its newspaper, the *Amerikanskij Russkij Viestnik*, though there were others as well.

Still another problem was the Roman Church which through the appointment of Bishop Basil was seeking to bring the "Greek Catholic Church" in the United States more into conformity with the Latin Rite churches responding to American Roman Catholic pressure. In Europe Bishop Basil had belonged to the most Hungarian and Roman-oriented group of clergy, who placed being "Catholic" ahead of being "Eastern." This would have dire repercussions in the years to come. In the United States a large group of Greek Catholic priests, especially those from Prjasevska Rus', were content to be "Uniates" but they viewed the Union agreements as contracts between themselves and the Roman See, and they felt that any "Latinization" was a violation of the contact. They were not interested in being "better Catholics" but being "Greek Catholics" as they had been in Europe.

It must be pointed out that the Roman See itself has always encouraged its "Greek Catholics" and the other

"Eastern Rites" in "union" with it to remain faithful to their "traditions" and strongly discourage (at least officially) any attempts at "Latinization," that is, to make the rites more similar to the Latin Rite. It often was the Uniates themselves, desiring to prove their fidelity to the Roman See and to gain the respect of the "Latins" (who frequently looked down on them as "second-class" members of the Catholic Church) who were the greatest Latinizers of all. This frequently produced a "hybrid" ritual of both Eastern and Roman elements.

By the time of Bishop Basil the "threat" of returning to Orthodoxy was not a large one, and had diminished greatly from the previous decade. The fateful events of 1917 ended any support for the Russian Orthodox Mission to America, the only jurisdiction that was viable for Carpatho-Russians at the time. (The amount of support was very much exaggerated in the Uniate Press.) The Russian Church in America in the 1920s was itself left in a state of disarray by the Russian Revolution; its capacity to do mission work hampered, and the living conditions of its clergy were worse than those in the Uniate Church.

Although initially the Uniate press rejoiced at having a bishop who was "one of us," their joy was short-lived as Bishop Takach failed to realize that the Uniate Church in America was not the Uniate Church in the "old country." Perhaps the greatest weakness of the bishop was the fact that he still clung to the Hungarian clericalism of the old country, still speaking the Hungarian language to the clergy and Carpatho-Russian only in a condescending way to the people. It was even rumored by some lay people that he could not speak "po nasemu" at all. Of course, this was not true. Even after eight years in the country, he still did not bother to become an American citizen, nor did he bother to learn the English language.[5] Of course, it should be pointed out that there were many priests who were equally delinquent on both counts. The Carpatho-Russian people in America, having breathed the air of freedom, found the clericalism of Bishop Takach and his advisors an odious reminder of the servitude to which they were held in Europe.

Although he claimed not to favor the clergy from one group over another, the facts seemed to prove otherwise. In 1923, before Bishop Takach had come to America, exactly half of the Carpatho-Russian officials of the diocese had attended the Presov Seminary from which also Gabriel Martyak, the diocesan administrator, had also graduated.[6] In 1924, after Bishop Takach's appointment, the breakdown was seven from Ungvar, four from Presov, and one priest who had attended the seminary in Budapest. The chancellor of the diocese under Bishop Takach was Theofil Zatkovich and the Rev. Julius Grigassy served as secretary; the former had attended the Budapest Seminary and the latter, who accompanied Bishop Takach from Europe, was a graduate of Uzhorod.[7]

Bishop Takach's handling of these appointments and even of parish assignments, where preference was given to the Uzhorod clergy, created a feeling of alienation among those of Presov and the few American-born priests. The trends that had been apparent in the seminary backgrounds of the priests in Europe were becoming apparent in America as well. The Presov group generally clung to the "Eastern Rite" and "Carpatho-Russian" or "Rusin" identity, viewing relations with the Roman Church through the terms of their "contract" with it, the Union of Uzhorod. They were Catholics but only because the union made them such; first they were "Eastern Rite." These clergy still continued in the tradition of living with "the people," though in America this meant learning English, becoming citizens, and in general accommodating themselves to the American way of life just as their parishioners were doing.

On the other hand, the Uzhorod group still moved towards assimilation, though no longer to the Hungarian dominant in Europe, though they still often favored the aristocratic Hungarian ways but rather to the dominant American Roman Catholic Church. Bishop Takach and his advisors were impressed with the immense power and wealth of the American Catholic Church and its control by the hierarchy. This for them was the role model, not the stubborn religious traditionalism of the Presov group.

From 1924-1929, the elements of a religious disaster were quietly being set in motion. In Europe there was a powerful set of controls, which like the control rods of a nuclear reactor kept the mass from reaching a critical level. But in America those controls, the lack of political and religious freedom, the geographical isolation between Presov and Uzhorod, the backward ways of village life, the lack of newspapers and other forms of communication, which kept the Uniate Church from coming apart were lacking. Every day the situation was growing critical. In 1929, the elements were triggered into a fiery explosion by a Vatican Decree entitled *Cum Data Fuerit*.

10. St. John's Carpatho-Russian Cathedral and Episcopal Residence in Artic Street, Bridgeport, Conn.

11. Bishop Soter Ortinsky — the first Greek Catholic
Bishop in America.

12. Masthead of the A R V.

13. The Rev. Orestes P. Chornock at age 32.

Chapter 4

A TIME TO CAST AWAY STONES

In the year 1929, Fr. Orestes Chornock, at the age of forty-seven, was seemingly at the height of his career as a priest. Saint John the Baptist Church on Arctic Street in Bridgeport was a large active parish, one of the largest in the American Greek Catholic Church and had become so under the leadership of Fr. Orestes. He was the dean of the New York Deanery of the Greek Catholic Diocese, a position which Bishop Takach had reconfirmed him in. He was financially quite well off. Yet by the end of the year 1930, Bishop Takach attempted to transfer him and threatened him with canonical suspension as a priest.

The trouble had started the previous year. On March 1, 1929, the Vatican authorities published a new decree, *Cum Data Fuerit,* with the purpose of regulating the Greek

Church in the United States internally and externally with its relationship with the American Catholic Church. The decree, which was to be in force for a period of ten years, outlined the duties and responsibilites of the bishop and clergy of the Greek Catholic Church, the immigration of priests, and the procedures to be followed in cases of "mixed rite" marriages. Except for one sentence it was hardly an innovative or radical document. The one sentence was to eclipse the whole of the document and begin the chain reaction that engulfed the Greek Catholic Church for almost a decade.

> "In the meantime, as has already been several times provided, priests of the Greek Ruthenian rite who wish to go to the United States of North America and stay there, must be celibates."

The provision for celibacy, as was stated in the decree, was nothing new. In fact in 1890 the Vatican attempted to insure that only celibate Greek Catholic priests would immigrate to America. The 1907, *Ea Semper* decree also restated that Greek Catholic priests in America were to be celibates. The lack of celibate priests caused the issue to be ignored by Bishop Ortinsky and overlooked by the Vatican. Bishop Takach continued to ordain married men to the priesthood, although by 1925 he had to have a special dispensation from the Vatican to do so. In 1927, Rome refused to grant a dispensation to this effect.[1] Perhaps sensing the problems that this would cause, Bishop Takach went to Rome in January 1928, to make his required episcopal report on the status of his diocese. Presumably the subject of a married clergy was also discussed. The events which followed revealed to the Roman authorities that they had made the correct choice in selecting Basil Takach to be the Greek Catholic Ruthenian bishop in the United States. His loyalty to the Roman Church, even against the interests of his own people, perhaps even against his better judgment, would preclude any attempt on his part to resist or ignore the issue of celibacy in America as his predecessor had.

On October 5, 1929, the decree *Cum Data Fuerit* was circulated among the clergy of the Pittsburgh diocese. However, even before it became "officially" known, the faithful of the Bridgeport parish had sent a delegation to Bishop Takach to find out his intentions in the matter of celibacy.[2] On September 18, 1929, they sent a petition to Bishop Takach asking him not to enforce celibacy.[3] The Bridgeport parish had a married seminarian who had completed his studies in Europe and would normally be ordained. However, under the conditions of *Cum Data Fuerit* the request for ordination would be categorically denied. Already on June 18, 1929, Fr. Orestes resigned from his deanship to protest Bishop Takach's plan to impose celibacy. Inquiring as to why seminarian Joseph Mihaly of the Bridgeport parish had been denied ordination, Fr. Orestes was told that it was none of his business and not to inquire further.[4]

As a result of this, on November 16, 1930, the eight Greek Catholic Union lodges of Saint John's parish in Bridgeport published a circular letter, in the newspaper *Rodina*, directed at the membership of both the Greek Catholic Union and the United Societies fraternal lodges, pointing out that enforcement of the celibacy provision of *Cum Data Fuerit* would mean that married seminarians, even though having completed their studies, would no longer be able to be ordained. The circular pointed out that celibacy was a violation of the Union of Uzhorod and called upon all Greek Catholics to protest to Bishop Takach.[5]

Ten days later, on November 26, 1930, Fr. Emil Nevicky, of Minersville, Pennsylvania, whose son-in-law, Basil Benyo, was denied ordination by Bishop Takach, was recalled to Europe by Bishop Paul Gojdic of Presov on the instigation of Bishop Takach because Fr. Nevicky had proposed that celibacy would be discussed by the clergy at an upcoming deanery meeting.[6] Bishop Takach, because of the recall order, denied Fr. Nevicky jurisdiction to function as a priest. After nine months of appealing, Bishop Takach with the support of his congregation, reconciled Fr. Nevicky after the latter had made an apology for "misconduct."[7]

The appearance of the circular letter in the newspaper *Rodina* incensed Bishop Takach and his advisors. In order to humiliate and to make an example for those who opposed his enforcement of the celibacy issue, Bishop Takach ordered Fr. Orestes Chornock transferred from Bridgeport, the largest parish in the diocese, to an insignificant parish in Roebling, New Jersey, even though Fr. Orestes was considered "Parochus" and an irremovable pastor.[8] This took place on December 11, 1930. Fr. Orestes' transfer was to take effect in twenty-four hours. On December 13, Fr. Orestes appealed to the bishop and requested canonical procedure in his case. On December 16, Bishop Takach denied the appeal and request for procedure and reiterated the order for transfer. On December 31, 1930, Fr. Orestes Chornock was notified that if he continued to celebrate the Divine Liturgy in the Bridgeport church, he would be suspended "ipso facto." That Sunday, Fr. Orestes had 375 people who had prepared to receive Holy Communion and attend the annual parish meeting which had been already announced. In view of the situation, Fr. Orestes celebrated the Sunday Liturgy. At the meeting his parishoners voiced their support for his position. On January 13, 1931, the official suspension of Fr. Orestes was published.[9]

The rest of the Greek Catholic community did not idly sit by and watch the situation in Bridgeport develop. Already on July 30, the directors of the Greek Catholic Union, meeting in Binghamton, New York, allowed for the use of the Union's funds to fight against celibacy.[10]

The Greek Catholic Union newspaper, the *Amerikanskij*

Russkij Viestnik, as in the days of Bishop Ortinsky, became the voice of protest in regard to the celibacy issue through the fiery articles of its editor, the Rev. Stephen Varzaly.[11] Fr. Varzaly, several years earlier in 1928, had been stricken with a throat ailment that impaired his power of speech. He was advised to go to the warm climate of Florida to recover.[12] In order to help Fr. Varzaly cover the expenses of such a trip, Bishop Takach requested a contribution from the priests of the diocese, himself contributing $200.00.[13]

Upon returning, Fr. Varzaly, through the influence of the bishop, became the editor of the *Amerikanskij Russkij Viestnik,* at the twentieth convention of the Greek Catholic Union held in June 1929. Fr. Varzaly, at the direction of the officers of the Greek Catholic Union, began writing against celibacy, which led to his suspension by the bishop. In an article that appeared in the *Amerikanskij Russkij Viestnik* on June 11, 1930 (no.24, p.1) he described the events of the early months of that year:

> Through the vote of the delegates of the Sojedinenije 20th, Gary, Indiana, Convention held in 1929, I became the chief editor of the *Amerikanskij Russkij Viestnik,* the official organ of the "Sojedinenije." The unexpected election of my person to the post of a chief editor of the *ARV* was a great honor and distinction.
>
> The important and responsible work of an editor of the *ARV* I took with great fear, hoping that God would help me. I began my work seriously and conscientiously. From the very beginning of my editorship, I worked with all my strength in the interest of the Sojedinenije, the Rusin people and the good of our Greek Rite Catholic Church.
>
> During my daily order of editorship, the question of celibacy came up. I had to occupy myself with the question on the pages of the *ARV* because this was demanded by my conscience . . . and by two special

resolutions of the Board of Trustees of the Sojedinenije.

The Board of Trustees of the Sojedinenije ordered me to write against celibacy and to protect the laws and privileges of our Eastern Rite. I, consequently, fulfilled the decision of the Board of Trustees precisely. In our organ I wrote several articles against celibacy and in defense of our laws and privileges of our Greek Rite Catholic Church of the Rusins.

My articles against celibacy did not please Bishop Basil Takach. On account of these articles, on April 23, 1931, Bishop Basil Takach took away from me permission to edit the *ARV*. Even in that I obeyed the order of the Bishop. He, to my surprise, suspended me on May 1, 1931 as a priest. When I expressed my disagreement in a letter, against the Bishop's attitude concerning my person, he decidedly reminded me to resign formally from the editorship of the *ARV* and see to it that my name was taken off the newspaper. I fulfilled the request of the Bishop when I resigned from the editorship of the *ARV* April 5, 1931.

Michael Yuhasz Sr., President of the Sojedinenije, who is also against celibacy in the interest of the Sojedinenije, did not accept my resignation, about which he notified me officially, saying, in the sense of the Sojedinenije by-laws, he had no right, no power, therefore he could not accept my resignation, because I only fulfilled the will of the board of trustees when I wrote against celibacy, defending the laws of our Greek Rite Catholic Church . . . .

Being that the Sojedinenije president did not accept my resignation, I am still the legal editor of the *ARV;* I am punctually in my office in Homestead, Pennsylvania in the Sojedinenije building. This is my obligation because I am responsible for all of the members of the organization, as I am the legal editor of the *ARV*.

Fr. Stephen Varzaly,
Editor of the ARV

The officers of the Greek Catholic Union upheld Fr. Stephen Varzaly as editor of the *Viestnik* despite his suspension. And his articles condemning celibacy, the Pope of Rome, and Bishop Takach continued. In response, Bishop Takach resigned his office as "Protector" of the Greek Catholic Union.[14]

The *Viestnik* responded with an attack on Bishop Takach, entitled "Persecution of the Faithful Sons of the Eastern Rite by Bishop Takach" on page four of the June 25, 1931 edition. The article was signed, "Old Priest," and was an emotional appeal for the preservation of the "Greek Rite Catholic religion," citing the progress of the last fifty years in America and lamenting that after having been given much cooperation and good will, Bishop Takach was now attempting to destroy the church through "Latinization" by imposing celibacy. The author claimed the Greek Catholic Union, the *Viestnik,* and Fr. Varzaly, editor of the latter, were only acting in the historical role of the Greek Catholic Union and its organ "to defend us from our enemies."[15]

Many of the clergy and faithful were deeply disappointed that Bishop Takach himself did not personally lead the fight against celibacy and Latinization but became the passive agent of Rome. Several of the priests had turned to Bishop Takach with the request that he protest the celibacy order. Though personally against its enforcement, the bishop refused and advised the priests to approach the Apostolic Delegate themselves, explaining to him the tragic consequences of the implementation of such an order.[16] If Bishop Takach had led the fight against celibacy, whatever would have eventually been the outcome, these chapters would have been written differently. As it turned out, despite the appeals of clergy and laypeople alike, Bishop Basil Takach was, in his own words, "always absolutely obedient" to the Roman See.[18]

The Trial of Fr. Orestes Chornock

The series of events that had happened in the early months of 1931 perhaps gave Bishop Basil cause to reflect that his suspension of Fr. Orestes Chornock, rather than having the desired effect of isolating him, was in fact making him a "confessor" of the Greek Catholic faith, while he, Bishop Takach, in the popular mind, was a persecutor of the church. On July 8th, Bishop Takach urged Fr. Orestes to take the proper steps for the suspension to be lifted.[19] Not wanting the stigma of suspension cast over his priesthood, Fr. Orestes, on August 5, 1931, requested that the suspension be lifted.[20] However, Fr. Orestes was unwilling to meet the terms of Bishop Takach: resign from the Bridgeport parish, and acknowledge his participation against the law of celibacy which Fr. Orestes denied. On August 18, Fr. Valentine Gorzo, one of Bishop Takach's most trusted advisors, initiated canonical proceedings against Fr. Orestes.

On August 30, 1931, the Lower Court convened by the diocese found Fr. Orestes guilty of "suscitationis turbarum, atque revolutionisinter fideles nostros, agitationis contra potestatis Ecclesiasticae"(exciting the crowds, of causing revolution among the faithful, of agitation against Church authority).[21] The sentence, despite the protest of four of the judges for clemency, was privation, the suspension of Bishop Takach being upheld.

On September 10, Fr. Orestes was informed of the verdict of the Lower Court. On September 20, he appealed on the grounds that there was a defect of procedure, since the court had been "stacked" with judges who were ardent supporters of Bishop Takach. The appeal also pointed out that according to the conditions of canon law the suspension was illegal since Fr. Orestes had appealed the transfer order. The appeal for canonical process in regards to the transfer order made him, at least temporarily, not liable for any punishment because he refused to obey it. The appeal also claimed that Fr. Orestes if not a "parochus inamovibilis"(irremovable pastor) was at least "parochus amovibilis," who could only be moved to a smaller parish for a serious offense by the bishop acting in accordance with the advice of at least two of the diocesan consultors and only after having been informed by the bishop and given an opportunity to correct the situation in question. The transfer of such a "parochus" could not be for punishment alone.[21] Bishop Takach ordered the transfer to punish Fr. Orestes and did so without the advice of any of the diocesan consultors.[22] The second trial of Fr. Orestes, to take place in Philadelphia before a Roman Catholic tribunal, was delayed until 1932. The tribunal was appointed by the Sacred Congregation for the Eastern Rites in Rome.[23] However, the year 1931 did not end quietly for Bishop Takach. This time, the trouble was not in far-away Bridgeport, but in Munhall, in his own cathedral church, with a young American-born priest, Fr. Peter Molchany, the assistant pastor of the cathedral.

Trouble in the Cathedral

Fr. Peter Molchany had already worked successfully for the diocese in Warren, Ohio and because of this, Bishop Takach transferred him to the parish in Clairton, Pennsylvania, which at the time was in the throes of a court battle. He lived for several months with his father-in-law in McKeesport until he was transferred to be the assistant to the ailing Fr. Alex Holozsnyay, the pastor of the cathedral parish.[24]

Fr. Peter Molchany was well-liked by the parishoners and when Fr. Holzsnyay was too ill to serve any longer, the parishoners elected him "pastor emeritus," provided him with a pension, and elected Fr. Molchany to be their pastor. This was done without the bishop's tacit permission, but Bishop Takach's silence was taken by all parties to mean that he in fact approved of the act. This took place on May 25, 1930.

On December 10, 1931, Bishop Takach, acting on the

advice of his consultors ordered Fr. Molchany transferred to Aliquippa. Such advice frequently caused a great deal of trouble for him since the consultors found Bishop Takach quite pliable and frequently manipulated him for their own ends. The cathedral congregation protested the action of Bishop Takach. However Fr. Molchany agreed to be transferred, and requested the Clairton parish to which he was originally assigned. The request was denied, as Bishop Takach had promised that parish to Fr. Michael Rapach, the son-in-law of Fr. Valentine Gorzo, one of the bishop's ardent supporters against Fr. Orestes Chornock, Fr. Varzaly, and the *ARV*.[25]

Since Fr. Molchany refused to comply with the transfer order, he was suspended on December 16, 1931 and was forbidden to hold any service in the cathedral. The bishop took out an injunction against the cathedral church, and the parishoners and Fr. Molchany were forced to celebrate the Christmas feastdays in a rented dance hall.[26] On January 12, 1932, the injunction was dissolved and Fr. Molchany and the parishoners again took possession of the church. This began a long court case that was not solved until 1934. The central issue of this case was not celibacy as in the others, but the Union of Uzhorod. Since the union stated that the bishop should be chosen by the clergy, Bishop Takach had no jurisdiction, it was argued, since he was not elected but appointed by Rome. The argument was advanced that in the case of the cathedral, the right of "jus patronatus" had been abrogated by the arbitrary actions of Bishop Takach in violation of the Union of Uzhorod. Bishop Takach, for his part, had already stated in a pastoral letter addressed to the clergy of the Pittsburgh Exarchate in May 1931 that obedience was the greatest virtue of the clergy, that Rome was not attempting to destroy the Greek Catholic Church but was only insisting on celibacy in the United States, that the Union of Uzhorod did not allow the Greek Catholics to dictate to the pope, and that the Union should have been made stronger in the past "to inject into our hearts the practical life, the request of Church authority, and the feeling of obedience." He called upon all the clergy to strengthen the discipline of the church and called upon those who were a part of the disorder to repair the harm done.[27]

1932 - The Conflict Intensifies

If 1931 ended on a bad note for Bishop Takach and his advisors with the problems in the cathedral, 1932 was off to no better a start. As we shall see, in many ways this year was marked by a solidification of those who were opposed to Bishop Takach and the enforcement of clerical celibacy and the rest of his policies.

Aside from the court battle for the cathedral, there were two events that were the harbingers of what was to come: the second trial of Fr. Orestes Chornock and the Greek Catholic Union Convention held from June 20 to July 2, 1932 in Detroit.

The Second Trial of Fr. Orestes

The second trial of Fr. Orestes took place before the Tribunal of the Philadelphia Archdiocese (Latin Rite) as directed by the Congregation for the Eastern Rites. However, from the outset the tribunal refused to admit any discussion of celibacy, or to examine the charges made by the defense that Bishop Takach was using the celibacy issue to further personal ends. The only thing to be discussed was the previous trial and the legality of the transfer ordered by Bishop Takach.[28]

The trial began on May 27 at 10:00 a.m. Fr. Orestes had selected Fr. Joseph Hanulya as his procurator and the Rev. Dr. Adrian Kilker served as his advocate. The brief for the defense stated that the previous trial was defective in its observance of canonical procedure, that Fr. Orestes was a "parochus" (pastor) who could not be moved except for grave reason, that the bishop did not follow

59

canonical procedure in the transfer, that Fr. Orestes had not incited the faithful to disobedience in the celibacy matter, that he could not be held responisble for the actions of the members of the Greek Catholic Union lodges in his parish, and that orderly protest is not grounds for a charge of disobedience and suspension. Fr. Hanulya pointed out that 125 priests of the Pittsburgh Eparchy had signed a petition against celibacy directed to the pope and the selection of Fr. Orestes for punishment on the grounds of orderly protest was unjust on the part of the bishop.[29] (Fr. Orestes did not sign the petition to Rome, which apparently had the blessing of Bishop Takach, though he himself did not sign it either. In the early years of the celibacy struggle, Bishop Takach was not opposed to the priests protesting celibacy to the Roman authorities in an orderly way, even though he himself would not join the protest. He was definitely opposed to the priests taking the struggle to the "people" through newspapers, articles, sermons, etc.)

The final sentence in the case of Fr. Orestes Chornock and Fr. Stephen Varzaly, who was also tried by the tribunal, was handed down on June 10, 1932. The defendants were found guilty as charged and were sentenced to be deprived of their office and position and forbidden to wear clerical clothing, forbidden to celebrate any liturgical services in the church, and deprived of all priestly privileges. The defendants were also obliged to pay all tribunal expenses.[30]

Bishop Takach communicated the results of the trial to his clergy and faithful in a pastoral letter on July 15, 1932. On July 21, 1932, Fr. Orestes appealed to the Holy Father, the pope, on the grounds that the Philadelphia Tribunal had not allowed sufficient time for the preparation of his case, for Fr. Hanulya wanted to delay the trial until May 31 but his request was denied. He had not been allowed to inspect the documents concerning the case and maintained that his transfer was not an administrative transfer but a penal one to which he was not canonically

60

subject. He appealed for "restitutio in integrum"—a full restitution.[31] The text of the appeal was carried in the *ARV* on July 28, 1932.

The 1932 Greek Catholic Union Convention

In March and April of 1932, Bishop Takach received communication from the Vatican concerning the deteriorating state of affairs in his diocese. On April 16, the Sacred Congregation for the Eastern Church responded to a petition sent by the priests of the diocese to Rome in regard to celibacy in September 1931. The response was directed to Bishop Takach and contained the following:

> The decree of the Congregation of the Propagation of Faith, namely that the priests who wish to come to America to exercise their ministry among the faithful of the Eastern Rite must be celibate, or, at least widowers, remains intact. This decree which notice was given to the bishops of the Latin Rite with a letter of April 12, 1894, referred to and refers to all priests without distinction between this or that rite . . . . Since the Holy Eastern Congregation did not reply to those Greek Rite priests of the city of Pittsburgh, who had sent a well-known petition to the Holy Father in September 1931. Considering the circumstances, a direct reply did not seem proper. I ask Your Excellency that on the next given occasion you be so kind as to notify the clergy, or at least those among the priests whom you deem more prudent, that the question of celibacy in America was again thoroughly discussed, and the Holy See has decreed that nothing be changed . . .[32]

The letter from the Vatican was made known to all the clergy of the diocese by Bishop Takach. However, many were unconvinced that it was the final word and were certain that a continued effort would bring results. The Greek Catholic Union Convention brought together the clergy and

61

laypeople in Detroit in June of 1932. This convention was completely anti-celibacy in tone. Bishop Takach had been requested to attend the Convention but declined, citing its disobedient anti-Roman atmosphere.[33]

The Convention proposed to send a petition protesting celibacy to high-ranking Roman Church officials both in the United States and in Rome. Many people felt that the problem did not lie with Bishop Takach but with his advisors who kept steering the bishop in the wrong direction on the matter of celibacy. A committee of five was appointed to meet with the bishop concerning the celibacy petition to see if his aid could be enlisted. The five-man committee of three priests and two laymen met with Bishop Takach on June 2, 1932 and then reported the next day that the bishop was inclined to cooperate in the matter with the Greek Catholic Union if the Greek Catholic Union would cooperate with him for "order and peace." Bishop Takach agreed to present the petition in Rome when he went to attend a bishop's conference, but would not guarantee its success. The questions of celibacy, the disposition of the suspended clergy, the ordination of the married seminarians could not be placed on the same petition, but would have to be presented separately. Bishop Takach insisted that the critical articles in the *ARV* to cease immediately to show the Vatican the good intentions of the Greek Catholic Union. Fr. Varzaly and Dr. Smor, the editors of the *ARV*, were to retract their articles which bordered on slander. Also, financial passive resistance had to cease. The churches had to fulfill their financial obligations to the diocese.[34]

Dr. Smor, Fr. Varzaly and others immediately refused to recall their articles on the grounds that they had spoken the truth. They felt in the words of Fr. Varzaly that the bishop had presented "impossible conditions" while Michael Yuhasz Sr., another author of anti-celibacy articles, felt that the bishop was trying to divide the people from their defending leaders, their "martyrs."[35]

On the other hand, Fr. Nicholas Csopey and Fr. Joseph Hanulya felt that to finally win the struggle would be impossible without the support of the Bishop. Both urged the convention to continue searching for a way to collaborate with the bishop who they felt "would act differently if he would not listen to one of his consultors but to the majority of the clergy."[36] The end result was the establishment of the Komiteta Oborony Vostocnoho Obrjada, "Committee for the Defense of the Eastern Rite," known by its Russian acronym "KOVO."[37] The members of the committee included both clerical and lay leaders of the Greek Catholic Church, including Fr. Orestes Chornock, Fr. Stephen Varzaly, and Fr. Peter Molchany, whose suspensions by Bishop Takach had only served to enhance their leadership capabilites as "Defenders of the Eastern Rite."

The Pamphlet of 1932

Immediately following the convention and the establishment of KOVO, a group of the clergy addressed a letter to Rome, outlining in detail the crisis situation that existed in the American Greek Catholic Church of the Pittsburgh Diocese. The rather lengthy document was addressed to the Pope and began with a review of the physical condition and the growth that had taken place in the diocese of Pittsburgh from its humble beginnings to the present day. That greater progress had not been made was laid to the fact that the diocese was subject to the Eastern Congregation in Rome, which was, they claimed, far removed from the spirit of Eastern Rite Catholicism. The pamphlet then reviewed the Union of Uzhorod which it claimed was a bilateral agreement that could not be altered without the consent of both parties involved. It furthermore stressed that the Union was not bound by geographical limitations, that where a "Greek Catholic Rite Rusin went so went with him the inherited rite and discipline of the Eastern Church."[38] The pamphlet continued to stress the three "rights" agreed upon at the Union of Uzhorod: 1) the use of the Eastern Rite,

2) a bishop elected by the clergy and approved by the Holy See (of Rome), and 3) the right to keep freely the church customs and discipline. The Union of Uzhorod and its interpretation were to play a major role in the events to come.

The pamphlet went on to attack Bishop Takach directly, citing that he had little concern for the spiritual life of the diocese but was only trying to demonstrate his "authority," especially in the matter of clerical transfers. The priests cited the bishop's introduction of the "Moleben to the Sacred Heart of Jesus Service" as a deliberate attempt to "Latinize" the Church. (Although devotion to the Sacred Heart of Jesus became popular in seventeenth century Roman Catholic circles, it is not to be found in traditional Eastern Christian theology and is in fact totally out of harmony with that theology.) Bishop Takach had improperly handled the construction of the episcopal residence and had failed to lead back the Orthodox "schismatics" to the fold of the Catholic Church, even though the condition of the Russian Revolution made this an ideal time to do so. Bishop Takach's thoughtlessness had created many court cases in the diocese and resulted in the loss of many churches. The reasons for the bishop's failure were his attachment to the old European ways, his selfishness, his tyranical attitude, and his advisors who manipulated him and to whom he owed favors.

The pamphlet continued to describe the introduction of celibacy, the suspensions of priests, the loss of the cathedral in court, and the establishment of the KOVO.

The priests cited a long list of decrees from popes, dating from the ninth century to the present, confirming the rights and privileges of the Eastern churches and seeking to demonstrate that they were in their rights. The priests acknowledged that many attacks were taking place that were anti-Roman and that the thread of unity was growing thin. They appealed to the pope to step in and restore the privileges of the Eastern Church and to curb the activities of those who were trying to "Latinize" it. The petition was signed by twenty-six of the leading priests of the Pittsburgh diocese, including Fr. Gabriel Martyak, who had been the administrator before Bishop Takach had been appointed, and Fr. Joseph Hanulya, the defense counsel at the trial of Fr. Orestes Chornock.[39] All were united against the policies of Bishop Takach.

In October of 1932, the Vatican forwarded through the office of the Apostolic Delegate in America an oath of obedience to the Roman Catholic Church and hierarchy, including their bishop and the observance of all canonical prescriptions issued by the hierarchy, notably the decree *Cum Data Fuerit* of 1929.

Many priests of the diocese forwarded a signed substitute oath, which they had composed, in which they swore obedience to the Holy See according to the terms of the Union of Uzhorod. They were basically the same group who sent the petition to the pope just described.[40]

The Fraternal Organizations—"Brother against Brother"

We have already seen the role of the Greek Catholic Union, the largest fraternal organization of the Carpatho-Russians, as the chief promoter against celibacy and Bishop Takach. Its newspaper, the *ARV,* edited by the suspended priest Stephen Varzaly, was a forum that reached into thousands of homes and after the 1932 Sojedinenije convention, the *ARV* carried an entire page devoted to the activities of the KOVO. It seemed that wherever there was a Greek Catholic Union lodge a KOVO chapter quickly sprang up.

There were two other fraternal organizations that were active among Carpatho-Russians as well, though neither had the large membership of the Greek Catholic Union. These organizations were the United Societies (Sobranije) and the Greek Catholic Carpatho-Russian Benevolent Association Liberty (Svoboda). Both of these organizations were in fact break-offs of the Greek Catholic Union.

65

The older of the two was the United Societies, which began when three of the Greek Catholic Union lodges of the Pittsburgh area met at Saint Nicholas Church in McKeesport, Pennsylvania on March 29, 1903, to form a new organization whose purpose was to provide "good leadership" which they believed was lacking in the Greek Catholic Union.[41] From this small beginning the organization experienced slow but steady growth. In 1908, Fr. Valentine Gorzo, a very "pro-Roman" priest became the spiritual advisor of the United Societies, a position he held until his death in 1946.[42] In the year 1919, the organization purchased the newspaper, *Prosvita* (Enlightenment), which became its official newspaper. Fr. Alexander Papp continued to edit the paper throughout the celibacy struggle. This priest reflected the attitude of Fr. Gorzo, that is, he was very pro-Roman and pro-Bishop Takach, which in the 1930s gave rise to the nickname for the newspaper of "Proslipa" (for the blind)! The articles in *Prosvita* were just as vehement as those in the *ARV*, except that they of course defended the bishop and celibacy.

The other organization, Liberty, was founded in July of 1918, under the guidance of Fr. Peter Kustan, the pastor of Saint John's Greek Catholic Church in Perth Amboy, New Jersey. The organizers of Liberty, like the organizers of the United Societies, were also dissatisfied with the Greek Catholic Union. The bulk of the membership of the Greek Catholic Union was to be found in the coal mining regions of Pennsylvania, where there were very high death rates and thousands of dollars in benefits paid out each year. The Eastern immigrants, in their factories, did not experience the same number of fatalities, yet they felt that their membership dues were making up the reserve capital of the organization. At convention time, since they were outnumbered, they had little voice in running the organization or in the handling of finances. For these reasons, despite hearty opposition from the Greek Catholic Union, the members of the Greek Catholic Union lodge of Saint John's Church in Perth Amboy formed the Liberty organization, which spread to other parishes in time,[43] though it would never rival the GCU in terms of membership. In August of 1919, Liberty began to publish its newspaper *Vostok* (The East). This newspaper was somewhat different than the other two in that it had a lay editor. There was also a clergy spiritual advisor. *Vostok* carried not only news of the events happening in the Uniate Church but also in Carpatho-Russia, and it even listed the activities that had taken place in the Russian Orthodox Church, such as ordinations to the priesthood, etc. In this regard it followed a much more independent policy than either the *ARV* or Prosvita, who despite their opposition of or support for Bishop Takach, continued to view the Orthodox as "schismatics."

The newspaper *Vostok* eventually did come out against celibacy and Bishop Takach, a policy that was no doubt reinforced by the court case in the Perth Amboy church. Liberty always had strong ties with the Perth Amboy church where it started and which stood across the street from the organization's headquarters. In fact, the October 17, 1935 edition of the paper bore the large headline "Pravda Pobidila" (The Truth Is Victorious) announcing the final decision in the Perth Amboy court case which Bishop Takach lost. The church was declared a trust of the congregation rather than of the Pittsburgh diocese. In fact the court proceedings were printed in that edition of the paper. Initially the leaders of Liberty felt that perhaps "church politics" were best left out of the organization, but the perceived threat to the "mother church" and the court case brought them out against celibacy and, of course, Bishop Takach.

Neither of these two organizations, the United Societies or Liberty, had the influence of the GCU simply because they did not have the large membership that the older organization had. As the struggle intensified, all of the fraternal organizations became eventually embroiled in it and their original purpose, of providing life insurance, faded into the background.

There were other organizations that were even smaller. The separate Russian Orthodox and Ukranian Brotherhoods, however, did not play the part in the struggle played by these other three.

1933—The Conflict Intensifies

The events of 1932, particularly the establishment of the KOVO, prepared the grounds for what was to come. In February of 1933, there were two events that foreshadowed the intensification of the conflict; the response of the pope to the appeals of Fr. Orestes Chornock and Fr. Stephen Varzaly and the call of the KOVO for an ecclesiastical congress to solve the problem of celibacy. The pope's response was as follows:

Apostolic Delegation, United States of America, 1811 Biltmore Street, Washington, D.C.

February 10, 1933 — No. 3796-i.
Reverend Orestes Chornock:
Reverend Sir:

The Sacred Congregation for the Oriental Church has received your request for "restitutio in integrum," sent on July 21, 1932, following the sentence of the Metropolitan Court of Philadelphia, given on June 10, 1932, which confirmed the sentence of the Diocesan Tribunal of your proper Ordinary.

The Sacred Congregation accurately examined all the acts of the process and decided, on January 7, with the approval of the Holy Father, to reject your request, because there were not sufficient motives to justify it.

Wishing you every blessing, I remain,
Sincerely yours in Christ,
P. Fumasoni Biondi, Abp. of Dolcea, m.p.,
Apostolic Delegate

Fr. Orestes Chornock's last attempt to vindicate himself in the eyes of the Catholic Church had just ended in failure. The issue of celibacy or the enforcement of *Cum Data Fuerit* was kept entirely out of his trial, without which it appeared to the Roman authorities as a simple case of disobedience. Fr. Varzaly received a similar response to his appeal. However, the suspended priests lost none of their authority and continued to be accepted by the bulk of Greek Catholics as priests who were in good standing, the victims of Bishop Takach's struggle to enforce the provisions of *Cum Data Fuerit*. They continued to serve in their parishes and to provide leadership. But since the appeal of Fr. Orestes was denied, the court case brought against him and the Bridgeport parish by Bishop Takach in February of 1932 continued.

Bishop Peter Bucys

Early in 1933 Pope Pius XI sent to the United States as his personal representative Bishop Peter Bucys, a Latvian, to attempt some sort of reconciliation in the celibacy controversy that had engulfed the Greek Catholic Diocese of Pittsburgh. Through his intervention, Bishop Takach lifted the suspensions of the three priests: Frs. Orestes Chornock, Peter Molchany, and Stephen Varzaly on April 10, 1933[44] on the condition that they obtain absolution in the external forum within sixty days; that is, that they publicly submit to the bishop and of course the policy of celibacy. Since none of the priests had done so at the end of the sixty days the suspensions remained in effect.[45] The *ARV* saw in Bishop Bucys someone whose stand was basically the same as Bishop Takach's.[46] After a stay of less than a year, Bishop Bucys left the United States without having accomplished this objective.

The Call to Arms

The KOVO page of the February 2, 1933 edition of the *ARV* issued a call for the organization of new KOVO chapters: "Organize KOVO branches in every place where there is none. Organize branches for after Pascha there will be a National Religious Congress, and if you wish to have your delegates at this congress you must have a KOVO branch."[47]

The "National Religious Congress" had been used before in the days of Bishop Ortinsky, and the KOVO directors believed that it would be effective again. The pages of the *ARV* for the first six months of 1933 were filled with advertisements for "vice" in different parts of the country where Greek Catholics were to be found. The "vice" was a kind of mass rally and a typical program would consist of several speakers, almost all of whom spoke "in defense of the Eastern Rite" (at least during the years of the celibacy struggle), perhaps some choral selections performed by one or more local choirs, often of church or "old country" folk music. This might be followed by an open discussion of the issues at hand. A "vice" held during the years in question was usually a highly charged emotional affair at which the affairs of the Greek Catholic Church were openly aired.

The local "vices" of 1933 culminated in a "Great Vice" held at the Nemo Theater in Johnstown, Pennsylvania, on June 11, which was to prepare the way for the "National Religious Congress" to be held in Pittsburgh the following month.[48] Fr. Stephen Varzaly, according to the *Johnstown Tribune,* made a highly emotional appeal for the defense of the "Eastern Rite."[49] The resolutions passed at the Johnstown vice called for the clergy to attend the KOVO "National Religious Congress" in July, especially members of the bishop's board of consultors. It called for a committee of priests and laypeople to administer the finances of the diocese in the interim until a new bishop could be secured.[50]

On June 6, 1933, the leaders of the KOVO met in Homestead at the GCU Offices to plan out the details and agenda of the "National Religious Congress." They comprised some twenty-two points that were to be brought out during the congress. Among them:

The National Religious Congress is to solemnly declare that neither the delegates nor those whom they represent want to leave Holy Mother Church. We do not want independence or schism, but we wish to remain the faithful children of the Greek Rite Catholic Church of the Eastern Rite united with the Holy Roman See. (Paragraph-Point 1)

We want the abrogation of celibacy. (Point 2)

We request a seminary and cantors school . . . (Point 6)

We request censure be definitely terminated from Fr. Stephen Varzaly, Fr. Orestes Chornock, and Fr. Peter Molchany. We also want the married seminarians ordained. (Point 10)

We request that the Church authority give out uniform religious and school books in Rusin and English. (Point 13) We are requesting that law processes be stopped which are still continued on account of some reasons in certain parishes, between the Church authority and the parish, the parish matters to be settled amicably and not in court.[51] (Point 20)

The date of the National Religious Congress was set for July 26, 1933 in Pittsburgh at the church hall of Saint John Chrysostom "Russian Greek Catholic" Church on Forward Avenue (a section of the city called "Rus'ka Dolina"). The Congress was to begin at 9:00 a.m. with a Divine Liturgy.[52]

Each KOVO branch was allowed to send two delegates plus the parish pastor. If the pastor refused to attend then three lay delegates were authorized. The delegates were to be certified by each chapter and the local priest if he was willing to sign the forms; if he wasn't the papers needed only the signature of the chapter officers.[53]

Bishop Takach Responds

On June 28 Bishop Takach released a notice to his clergy in which the upcoming National Religious Congress was indirectly labeled as being "In the domain of radicalism" and ordered all of the clergy to refrain from either attending or participating in it, warning of the consequences.[54]

The Program of the Congress

The program of the Congress, released in June of 1933, included many highly respected lay people and, despite the threats of the bishop, many clergy as well. Among the clerical speakers was Fr. Gabriel Martyak, the former administrator of the Pittsburgh diocese before the appointment of Bishop Takach; Fr. Stephen Varzaly, the suspended editor of the *ARV*; Fr. Joseph Hanulya, a well-known figure in Carpatho-Russian circles, a celebrated defender of the "Eastern Rite" and "Rusin" nationality and the choice of Fr. Orestes Chornock as his "defense attorney" at his church trial; Fr. Alexius Vislocky, the spiritual advisor of the Liberty "Svoboda" organization; Michael Yuhasz, the chairman of the KOVO; Dr. George Varga, the vice-president of the GCU; as well as John Popp, the president of the GCU "Sokols."[55]

Among the items on the agenda was a proposed visit to Bishop Takach by a selected committee as well as the reading of his reply to the committee if any such reply was forthcoming.

The Resolutions of the National Religious Congress of 1933

The October 5, 1933 edition of the *ARV* carried the following resolutions of the KOVO at the National Religious Congress. These were forwarded to the Pope Pius XI in Rome. The text of this document was sent to the Vatican in August.

To His Holiness, the Pope of Rome, Pius XI.
Vatican City.

Your Holiness:

On July 27-27-28, 1933 we held in Pittsburgh, Pa., United States of America the Religious National Congress of the Greek Rite Catholics of the Pittsburgh Eparchy. Representing the parishes and the people were present 311 delegates, 45 priests and 60 cantors.

This Congress was the culmination of a three-year-old battle for the preservation of our rights and privileges, a battle which is fast destroying the religious and moral life of a half-million Carpatho Rusin Greek Rite Catholics in America, and which is detrimental to the Catholic Church in general by focusing the attention of all non-Catholics to our sorry plight and to the unmerciful and unjust administration of the Carpatho Rusin Greek Rite Catholic Church in America united with Rome.

The purpose of calling this Congress was put into concrete-form the demands of the American Greek Rite Catholics of the Greek Rite Catholic Eparchy of Pittsburgh, PA., to restore order and to make secure its future welfare.

This Congress decided that the undersigned, as a committee selected for that purpose, sent to the Roman See and to the Apostolic Delegate at Washington, D.C., a copy of the enclosed resolutions of the said Religious National Congress.

For that reason, we as a committee as above set forth transmit and herewith enclose the resolution as adopted by the religious National Congress of the Carpatho Rusin Greek Rite Catholics in America united with Rome.

Signed this 14th day of August, 1933, by the Executive Committee of the Religious National Congress at the Carpatho Rusin Greek Rite Catholics of America.

Most Humbly Yours,

Stephen Sterenchak   Rev. Stephen Varzaly
Peter Korpos   John Furda
John Lois   Andrew Hleba
Rev. Peter Molchany   Dr. George Varga
George Jogan

RESOLUTIONS

Par. l. We stand firmly by the covenants of the Union of Uzhorod--Ungvar, entered into the year 1646, and we demand that the Roman See observe the conditions of said Union of Ungvar and the inviolability of the Eastern Rite.

2. We demand that celibacy and Latinization be recalled from the Eastern Church in the United States of America, once and for all times.

3. We demand the recall of Bishop Basil Takacs and his cabinet. If this not be done, then we will forthwith cease to pay the cathedraticum. We do not acknowledge him as our bishop.

4. We demand that penances, suspensions and excommunications be lifted immediately from all priests and laymen in our Eparchy, that peace may be restored among the clergy and the people.

5. We demand that immediate ordination of our present married seminarians, who have completed their studies, and also at the proper time of those who in the future shall fulfill the will and requirements of our Eastern Greek Rite Catholic Church.

6. We demand that in accordance with the terms of the Union of Ungvar, a bishop or an administrator, who is a citizen of the United States of America, be elected from among our American Rusin clergy.

7. We demand that we have our representatives in the Congreation of the Eastern Rite, who shall be chosen from among the American Rusin priests in America.

8. We demand, beginning today, our name be Carpatho Rusin, instead of "Ruthenian" of the United States.

9. We demand that our Eparchial By-laws be made for the whole Pittsburgh Eparchy, regulating both the clergy and the cantors, their rights, salaries and stole, as well as the whole school system. The Congress shall nominate two priests, two cantors and five civilians who are to compile the By-laws.

10. We demand that all church property be recorded in the name of the parish, that neither the bishop, nor the priest be trustee, that only the parishioners, not fewer than five in number, shall hold these offices.

11. We demand that no parish shall pay a priest who opposes and work against the rights and privileges of the Greek Rite Catholic Church.

12. In the event that the Roman See be not inclined to respect our rights, which were guaranteed to us by the Union of Ungvar in the year 1646, and does not take into consideration the demands of this Congress within sixty days, we, all the people, together with our churches and the clergy shall break relations with the Roman See for so long a time as our demands are not acknowledged, that is, we shall become independent from Rome.

Fr. Joseph Hanulya wanted to protest against several of the paragraphs of the Resolutions, however the National Religious Congress would not give him the opportunity to present his arguments. (In 1932 Fr. Hanulya and the other clergy who had not been suspended by Bishop Takach for their anti-celibacy activities resigned from the executive board of the KOVO, for fear of suspension since the bishop

74

had forbidden the clergy to serve on the board of the KOVO.)[56] The resignations caused many of the lay people to feel abandoned and needless to say the popularity of those who resigned declined considerably. Although bitterly opposed to celibacy and Latinization Fr. Hanulya was in his heart a staunch son of the Roman Church (as events will show). Since he was not allowed the floor his disagreements with the accepted resolutions were entered into the minutes of the Congress in the form of a letter:

The Opinion of the Clergy to the presented resolutions of the Congress Committee

In the resolutions the clergy found the following paragraphs not legal and contradictory.

1. If we are firmly standing by the Ungvar Union of 1646 as it is stated in the first paragraph, . . . then we cannot logically and justly so accept the one we asked for, who is appointed by — the Roman See and by us in spite of this that he was not elected — by the clergy in 1924, . . . the accepted bishop will stay until Rome recalls him.

2. True, . . . to prevent the Ungvar Union conditions, the clergy may willfully use it as it appears in the request in the 6th paragraph, then the bishop or administrator cannot be freely elected, and if it is done so, then morally it destroys the right to choose a person (Example, Hodermarsky).

3. To appoint members to the different Congregation, that is exclusively the right, authority of the Pope of Rome himself. For the clergy to demand, that they without a special permission elect a representative in the Holy Congregation, as it is mentioned in paragraph 7, that is taking away the right from the Pope of Rome.

4. Paragraph 10. that the bishop and the clergy should not be trustees of the church, in many states that is contrary to the state law. Such a decision would place the Congress as one ignoring the state law, what should never

75

happen.

5. This struggle was not, nor is it a struggle between the clergy and people, but a struggle to revoke celibacy and Latinization. Not to pay the salary of the priests until they will not make order, as the 11th paragraph proposes, is illogical and unjust, and a punishment for the fighters for the Eastern Church.

In such an attitude the Congress is overstepping its trust, authority, pledge (vidi. the invested power). If they would accept this, what is proposed in the 12th paragraph, i.e. that we all with our churches break relations with the clergy and the Roman Apostolic See. With this we would destroy even the good proposals. The clergy are protesting against such proposals, and the acceptance of them. These resolutions not only would not be victorious, but instead the Congress would destroy the whole matter.

Rev. Joseph P. Hanulya   Rev. Michael Morris
Rev. Vladimir Mihalics   Rev. Orestes Chornock
                    Rev. Michael Staurovsky

In this letter Fr. Hanulya and his co-signers, among them the suspended Fr. Orestes Chornock, sought to uphold the rights of the Roman see in the American Greek Catholic Church. They believed that the solution to the problems of the church lay in collaboration with the church authorities. As we have stated earlier many expected Bishop Takach to lead the fight against "Cum Data Fuerit" as Bishop Ortinsky did against *Ea Semper* and as late as 1933 still believed that it was only because Bishop Takach had surrounded himself with the "wrong" advisors that he was not leading the fight. Through the early 1930s there were many appeals to Bishop Takach to take the lead in the fight; when it became apparent through his reaction to the National Religious Congress of 1933 that he would not have anything to do with the KOVO the struggle was taken to the Vatican.

The Response of Bishop Takach

On July 30, 1933, on the heels of the congress, Bishop Takach sent a letter to Michael Yuhasz Sr., the president of the GCU under whose wing the KOVO operated. In this letter Bishop Takach pointed out the shame that the ultimatums contained in the Resolutions of the Congress had brought to the Pittsburgh Eparchy. He questioned the presence of "schismatics" at the congress, which purported to be a congress of the Greek Catholic Church. Since according to church law such a congress could only be called by a bishop, Bishop Takach declared the congress and its resolutions as null and void, and urged the GCU to heal the wounds caused by this tactless move.[57]

The Clergy Conference of August 1933

Bishop Takach did not limit his response to a formal letter to the executives of the GCU. He summoned the priests of the Eparchy to Pittsburgh to attend a conference that would deal with the crisis brought on by celibacy. (Since Frs. Orestes Chornock, Peter Molchany, and Stephen Varzaly were suspended they were, of course, not present. However many of the anti-celibacy clergy were). The minutes of this meeting show that there was a general "airing out" of the problem. The ultimatum of independence contained in the Resolutions put many of the clergy in a difficult position. They were opposed to celibacy but realized that they could not function as priests without a bishop. The threat of leaving the fold of Rome and forming an "Independent Greek Catholic Church" contained in the resolutions was not a new threat; it had been previously made as far back as 1891.[58] Never had the possibility of it happening become so real though and to many of the clergy this was frightening.

Bishop Takach justified his refusal to attend the 1932 Convention in Detroit, where the KOVO was started, by saying that his presence was forbidden since there was agitation against the Holy See.[59] Bishop Takach felt that the position of Rome on the celibacy issue was contradictory to the Union of Uzhorod and he urged the clergy to once more send a petition "from the heart" asking for its repeal with the promise of perpetual obedience on the part of the Greek Catholic clergy of the Eparchy.[60] Fr. Michael Staurovsky, a clergy signer of the resolution, repudiated his signature before the clergy and the bishop and Fr. Joseph Hanulya condemned the KOVO for its objectives and goals.[61]

The clergy issued several documents directed to the GCU and to the faithful of the Pittsburgh Eparchy, condemning the actions and resolutions of the "National Religious Congress" and urging the people to follow the leadership and to respect the authority of the Pope of Rome together with that of the bishops and priests.[62] The letter to the faithful also promised that new diocesan statutes would be promulgated.[63]

The letter to the GCU urged that organization not to assist the KOVO, that its officers abandon their leadership of the KOVO, and that the KOVO page not be published in the *ARV*.[64] Furthermore it stated that the clergy did not recognize the KOVO "National Religious Congress" and declared all of its resolutions void.[65] The letter was signed, as was the letters to the faithful communicating the same information, by the priests of the eparchy who were present at the clergy conference, including those who previously were opposed to "celibacy" and "Latinization" such as Fr. Joseph Hanulya, Fr. Gabriel Martyak, and Fr. Orestes Koman among others.[66] The clergy resolved to petition the Holy Father to repeal the celibacy provision of "Cum Data Fuerit" and thereby to make peace in the diocese.[67]

Bishop Takach, in a pastoral letter of September 1, 1933, related the response of the GCU to his letter of July 30. The GCU officers denied that they were sowing discord and further denied that any "schismatics" had taken part in the National Religious Congress. They again urged Bishop Takach to take up the fight to safeguard the Eastern Rite and placed any failure on his part to do so as the cause of the problem. Bishop Takach, in light of this reply, called upon the clergy to take a stand against the KOVO and the GCU and to let that stand be known. He wrote: "The Roman See is holding on to its standpoint. There is no other way before us but to obey." He further expressed his belief that the majority of the clergy and at least fifty to sixty percent of the faithful were loyal to the Catholic Church and would not tolerate schism or independent existence. He urged that the clergy take the lead against the KOVO and its threat of an independent church.[68] Many priests were sitting on the fence between the bishop and the KOVO, not wishing to be afoul of either one. As the intensity of the struggle increased these priests found that they would have to make a choice: both the bishop and the KOVO were demanding their support.[69]

An Evaluation of the Events of 1933

Instead of bringing a resolution to the conflict, the year 1933 saw the Greek Catholic Pittsburgh Eparchy polarized into two groups; the KOVO and its chapters on one side, together with the suspended priests Orestes Chornock, Peter Molchany, and Stephen Varzaly, still functioning as the editor of the *ARV,* as its spiritual leaders and bishop Basil Takach and the bulk of the clergy of the eparchy, along with (by Bishop Basil's own estimate) fifty to sixty percent of the faithful. Several reasons have been proposed for the so-called celibacy struggle besides the issue of celibacy itself. Among them the desire of the GCU to keep its members occupied with the fight so that they would not notice the internal financial problems of the organization, the desire of Bishop Takach to end the "trustee system" of holding church property and to have the diocesan bishop as the chief trustee, as per normative American Catholic practice and, finally, the personal ambitions of the clergy dissatisfied with Bishop Takach and desirous of regaining control of the eparchy.

The depression of 1929 was the source of a great deal of financial difficulty for the GCU. The organization had, in one instance, $200,000.00 invested in a Johnstown bank, of which the GCU treasurer at the time was an officer. When the bank was forced to close its doors the entire amount was lost.[70] This was a staggering blow to the organization. The state of New York questioned the solvency of the GCU in the aftermath of this and the organization was no longer allowed to collect dues there. In 1932, the state of Pennsylvania forced the GCU to adopt the rate premiums of the "American Experience System" which raised the rates so much that many of the older members were almost forced out of the Union.[71] It has been alleged that the GCU officers seized the celibacy issue to draw attention away from the problem of its finanical solvency, and to rally its members.

Certainly the celibacy issue served as a rallying point for members of the GCU, however the allegation that the GCU manipulated the celibacy issue to its own purposes is a questionable one on two counts. First, the organization was deeply split on the handling of its financial difficulties as is revealed by its 1932 Convention held in Detroit— the same convention that gave birth to the KOVO. As mentioned above the state of Pennsylvania gave an ultimatum to the GCU to adopt the "American Experience System" or cease its operations there. The Detroit Convention of 1932 saw this proposed on the floor of the convention and the final vote regarding its adoption is very revealing: 228 in favor and 224 opposed.[72] The ability of the GCU to operate as an insurance organization was saved by only four votes! Yet in the face of this deep division the KOVO received the support of virtually every local chapter of the GCU in organizing a local branch. Although divided on internal policy in regards to insurance the GCU presented a united stand "in defense of the Eastern Rite." There is another problem with the allegation that the GCU

80

manipulated the celibacy issue to cover its financial difficulties. The National Religious Congress, which framed the ultimatum sent to Rome on the celibacy issue, took place in July of 1933 through the promotional activities of the KOVO and the *ARV* newspaper, the offical organ of the GCU. However, the January 12, 1933 edition of the *ARV*, in banner red headlines, proclaimed that the GCU was 100% solvent and spoke of the great progress made since the difficultities of the 1932 Convention.[73] If the organization was solvent, what purpose could it have in prolonging the struggle over celibacy, which would finally prove against its best interests, as we shall see. The Detroit 1932 Convention of the GCU would seem to reveal that despite the celibacy issue the organization was still internally divided and, in fact, over the next ten-year period would come to terms with Bishop Takach.

By taking the stand that it did in the "Latinization struggle," the GCU was carrying out its own perceived image as the "guardian of the Greek Catholic People" against all those who sought to destroy them. This was in the "tradition" of the GCU from almost its inception and we need only recall the role it played in the conflicts with Bishop Ortinsky and the "Ea Semper" decree. The GCU and the dependent KOVO organization saw themselves as defenders of the Eastern Rite; they continually sought the aid of Bishop Takach to lead the struggle and it was only after it became apparent that he refused to do so that they called for his removal, as is revealed in the documents of the period.[74]

Ambition of Bishop Takach

Another reason given for the struggle over celibacy and "Latinization" is the desire of Bishop Takach to gain control of all the parish properties, which in the majority of instances were governed by a system of lay trustees. Since many lay people had mortgaged their homes to provide capital to build the churches and since there was very

81

little church authority to oversee the building and chartering of churches (often a church was built without authorization from anyone and then attempts were made by the
parishoners to obtain a priest), they were often chartered
as non-profit religious organizations. Bishop Takach did
attempt to rectify this irregular situation. However, many
of the churches in question did mention that they were
"united with Rome" in their charters and others were
chartered under the authority of the local Roman Catholic
bishop. It would appear that the greatest obstacle to
uniform chartering of all the churches with the bishop as
the trustee (as per normal Catholic practice) was Bishop
Takach himself. His weak stand on the celibacy and
"Latinization" issue revealed him to many Greek Catholics
as a person who could not be trusted, a "traitor" to the
Greek Catholic Church.

The preparatory meeting of the KOVO board for the
"National Religious Congress" recommended that the
following be considered as the first point in the program
of the Congress:

> The National Religious Congress is to solemnly declare
> that neither the delegates not those whom they repre-
> sent do not want to leave Holy Mother Church, do not
> want Independence nor Schism, but wish to remain
> faithful children of their Greek Rite Catholic Church of
> the Eastern Rite united with the Holy Roman See.[75]

The resolutions produced by the Congress and sent to
Rome reflect the lack of trust in Bishop Takach and sought
to safeguard the churches, not from episcopal authority,
but from any future betrayal into the hands of the
"Latinizers." Had Bishop Takach taken the lead in the fight
against celibacy, instead of accepting whatever came from
the Vatican without a protest and sitting on the sidelines
whenever his priests protested, in short, if he revealed
himself as a "defender of the Greek Catholic Church" and

sought to cultivate the trust of the faithful regardless of the final outcome of the struggle, the problem of church charters could have been easily resolved.

A third reason has also been given for the celibacy struggle: the personal ambitions of the clergy who were dissatisfied with Bishop Takach who wished to regain control of the diocese. This charge has been specifically leveled at Fr. Orestes Chornock. To be sure, there were individuals who used the celibacy struggle for their own advantage. There are records of priests who drifted back and forth between the Uniates and the Orthodox, with loyalty only to themselves. Orestes Chornock, as the facts reveal, was not one of these. His concern was not for himself but for his people. Despite Bishop Takach's favoritism toward the "Uzhorod clergy"(see p. 41), Fr. Orestes Chornock had no initial quarrel with him. In the years before 1929 Bishop Takach had visited the Bridgeport parish and, indeed, Fr. Orestes Chornock had been reappointed by him as the dean of his deanery.

The initial issue in Fr. Orestes' conflict with Bishop Takach was not based on any personal clash or power struggle. In his position as dean, and as the pastor of Saint John the Baptist, one of the largest Greek Catholic churches in America, Fr. Orestes was in a position of authority in the church. He had everything to lose and nothing to gain from any conflict with the bishop. Fr. Orestes simply sought to see his seminarian ordained a priest according to the tradition of the Greek Catholic Church, something that Bishop Takach refused to do.

The attempted intercession of Fr. Orestes on behalf of Joseph Mihaly, the seminarian in question, with Bishop Takach reveals the great concern of Fr. Orestes for his people, and for the tradition of his church. He could have simply dropped the matter, told his seminarian that there was nothing he could do and without doubt that would have been the end of the affair. But Fr. Orestes was willing to risk his entire priesthood for the sake of his people and their church.

Nor was Fr. Orestes initially anti-Roman; he together with Fr. Hanulya and several other priests signed the letter entered into the minutes of the 1933 National Religious Congress protesting those resolutions that infringed on the authority of the pope and the bishop and also protesting the twelfth article, the threat to leave the Roman Church as overstepping the authority of the Congress.[76]

Like Fr. Toth before him, it was no desire to lead a rebellion against the legitimate church authority that prompted Fr. Orestes to become the leader in the fight against celibacy and Latinization and the subsequent return to the Orthodox Church. Rather it was the realization that the church authority betrayed the trust and the faith of the people through "Latinization," and that it was only in the Orthodox Church that that trust and faith could find free expression again.

The Pamphlet "Our Stand"(Nase Stanovisce)

The year 1934 saw a great deal attention focused on the Union of Uzhorod and the conditions of the Union. The KOVO and the GCU, along with their spiritual leaders, Frs. Orestes Chornock, Peter Molchany, and Stephen Varzaly, as well as many other priests of the Pittsburgh Greek Catholic Diocese, maintained that the Union of Uzhorod was a bilateral contract between the then Orthodox Carpatho-Russians and the Catholic Church and that among the terms of the contract were the inviolability of the "Greek Rite" (including the ordination of married men to the priesthood and the preservation of the Orthodox spiritual tradition), the election of a candidate for bishop by the clergy with Papal confirmation, and that all of the political and social privileges of the Latin Rite clergy would be extended to those of the Greek Rite.[77] Those opposing "celibacy and Latinization" insisted on the bilateral character of the Union of Uzhorod and in fact viewed it as the very foundation for the existence of their "Greek

Catholic Church" and felt that any changes made in the agreement had to be consented to by both of the contracting parties. That is, before it could introduce celibacy in the United States, the Roman Church had to have the agreement of the Greek Catholic Church. They also pointed out that since Bishop Takach had not been elected by the clergy, according to the terms of the Union but appointed by Rome, his jurisdiction was questionable.

On the other, the United Societies and the clergy loyal to Bishop Takach sought to discredit the Union of Uzhorod and deny its terms. In a series of articles in the newspaper *Prosvita* appearing in 1934 the two-sided character of the Union of Uzhorod was denied, as well as the three conditions of its acceptance. Even the existence of the Union of Uzhorod, as a written document, was denied. (As a point of fact no one could produce the actual document of the Union which was either lost or may have never been recorded, although there is sound historical evidence that such a union did take place.)[78] The question essentially became, "What is the nature of Greek Catholic Church?" Is it a church "united to Rome" through an external contract or is it, in fact, an integral part of the Roman Church, merely celebrating under the tradition of the "Greek Rite?"

In 1934, through the offices of the GCU, was published a pamphlet reprinting articles that had appeared in the *ARV* in defense of the bilateral character of the Union of Uzhorod and its conditions, written by Dr. Peter Zeedick and Adalbert Smor. The pamphlet was entitled *Nase Stanovisce (Our Stand)* and presented the defense of the Union of Uzhorod and its terms of agreement, attempting to refute the claims of the newspaper *Prosvita,* in great detail. The work gave an overview of the history of the Greek Catholic Church in the United States and the opposition to it found among many of the Latin bishops. The authors went on to recall that Bishop Ortinsky had signed the resolutions of the National Religious Congress of 1913 which in articles 24 and 25 called upon the bishop to ordain married men to the priesthood according to the tradition of the Church and to protect and defend the "Greek Rite Catholic Rusin Church."[79] Unlike Bishop Takach, the authors stated, "We do not believe we have the right to exist only if we receive the approval of our existence from the part of the Roman Catholic clergy . . ."[80]

The pamphlet went on to define "Rite" as including not only liturgical tradition but also the entire life of the church. In the case of the Greek Rite it included not only the Greek liturgies, but also the marriage of the clergy and the Julian calendar. The work brought out the fact that "Latinization" in fact did not begin recently but had been slowly and steadily taking place in Europe almost immediately on the heels of the Union of Brest-Litovsk and Uzhorod. They cited the "Latinizations" of the Greek Rite approved at the Synod of Zamosc in 1720[81] as well as other instances.

In addition to the threat from Latinization, Zeedick and Smor also saw a threat from the "Ukrainian" movement that would attempt to destroy the Carpatho-Russian nationality of the people and replace it with a Ukrainian one. They alleged that the agents of the Ukranian movement were using the Uniate Church to further their aims. The celibacy struggle was a struggle against both Latinization and Ukrainization. The authors urged the election of a bishop by the clergy and even the use of English in the Liturgy as means of overcoming these threats and insuring the survival of the Greek Catholic Church.

The Reply of Rome to the KOVO Resolutions

In July of 1934, the Vatican authorities finally responded to the KOVO resolutions by way of the Apostolic Delegate. The reply was made known only to the priests of the diocese by Bishop Takach, with a request that its contents be kept from the faithful.

From the Bishop of the Greek Rite Diocese of Pittsburgh.

Homestead, Pa.

No. 263-1934
To the Reverend Clergy of the Diocese!

My Beloved Sons and Brothers in Christ:
I have recently received the decision of the Holy See on the question of celibacy, as communicated to His Excellency, the Apostolic Delegate, by the Sacred Congregation for the Oriental Church. It is my duty to communicate the entire letter of the Sacred Congregation to the Reverend clergy.

Sacred Oriental Congregation.
Prot. No. 572-30

Rome, July 23, 1934
(Borgo, Nuovo, 76.)

Your Excellency:
It is certainly not without profound pain that the Holy See has had to realize that, among the Catholics of the Greek Ruthenian Rite in the United States of America, and in particular among the clergy and faithful of the Pod-Carpathian Ruthenian Ordinariate, grave agitations and deplorable rebellions are being intensified and expanded on the pretext that this Sacred Congregation had threatened the rights and privileges of the Ruthenian Church.

But your Excellency knows well how, under the appearance of vast questions, there lies prevalently that much more restricted question, which has its origin in the regulation of article XII of the Decree *Cum Data Fuerit* of March 1,1929, and by which was again decreed what had already been prescribed since 1890; that is to say, "that Greek Ruthenian priests who desire to betake themselves to the United States of America and to remain there must be celibates." This regulation indeed was not and is not a "lex de coelibatu apud clerum graeco-ruthenum," as some have wanted to affirm. By it, nothing has been modified or changed in that particular Ruthenian ecclesiastical discipline, to which, in so far as it concerns the privilege of a married clergy, the Holy See has consented and still does consent. This regulation arose not now, but anew, from the peculiar conditions of the Ruthenian population in the United States of America. There it represents an immigrant element and a minority, and it could not, therefore, pretend to maintain there its own customs and traditions which are in contrast with those which are the legitimate customs and traditions of Catholicism in the United States, and much less to have there a clergy which could be a source of painful perplexity or scandal to the majority of American Catholics.

And, moreover, when the Holy See recognized the peculiarities of the Greek Ruthenian Church and guaranteed them, it intended principally—as is evident from the Decree of Union of 1596, during the Pontificate of Clement VII, and of the Brief of Paul V of 1615—to recognize and guarantee the ritual traditions of the Ruthenians.

87

As regards their particular canonical discipline, the Holy See could not have affirmed its integral application at all times and in all places without taking into account the different exigencies and circumstances. Thus one can well understand how a married clergy, permitted in those places where the Greek Ruthenian Rite originated and constitutes a predominant element, could hardly be advisable in places where the same Rite has been imported and finds an environment and mentality altogether different.

Let it not be said that the regulation of *Cum Data Fuerit* was new legislation, since the preceding Decree *Cum Episcopo (August 17, 1914)* —issued as a modification of the Constitution *Ea Semper (June 14, 1907)* —did not make any mention of it.

The fact that no mention was made of it in the Decree *Cum Episcopo* was not due in any way to a revocation of the regulation, adopted since 1890 and solemnly called to mind on several occasions; on the contrary, it was due to an indulgent attitude of the Holy See taken in view of the statements of the Ruthenian Bishops in Europe to the effect that the number of unmarried priests in their dioceses was still too few and that they could not very well reduce that number by asigning some of them to the spiritual assistance of the Ruthenian faithful in America. And that this was so is proven clearly by the fact that in the years from 1914 to 1929—that is during the period in which the regulation in question did not appear—the Holy See upheld in practice the same regulation, which continued to be known to the entire Ruthenian hierarchy and clergy so much so that when the Ordinary of the Pod-Carpathian Ruthenians in the United States of America deemed it necessary in 1925 to ordain some married clerics, he asked the Holy See to permit him, by way of exception to do so. The Holy See in acceding to the request, took care to emphasize the exceptional nature of the permission and to add "exclausa quavis spe futurarum ordinationum."

As the situation changed for the better, it seemed well that the decree of March 1, 1929, should state again, explicitly, that which in fact had never been abrogated. And so much the more so, because the regulation in question does not concern exclusively the Ruthenian clergy, but applies without exception to priests of all Rites.

But the Decree was accompanied on the part of the Holy See by an attitude of the greatest discretion and indulgence; so that even after it, no action was taken to send away from the United States those married Ruthenian priests who had already immigrated there in opposition to the regulation which would have forbidden them to do so; and these priests were not disturbed even when some of them showed themselves to be partisans of an altogether deplorable movement of hostility against their bishop and against the Holy See itself.

In the face of the simplicity and the logic of what article XII of the Decree *Cum Data Fuerit* disposes, it seemed immediately evident that some sought to bemuddle the situation, deceiving the ingenuous minds of the faithful by a misleading and a malign interpretation of every act emanating from the Holy See and put into effect by the Ordinary, Bishop Takach. And if there would have been any doubt about this, it would have been dissipated at lengths by what happened in the Convention, promoted by the KOVO and held in Pittsburgh from July 26 to 28, 1933: a meeting of intents and manifestations clearly schismatic, even to the extent of threatening the Holy See that unless it had—within sixty days—granted what was requested in the resolutions of the convention, the delegates at Pittsburgh and the people whom they represented would declare themselves "independent of Rome." A tremendous statement, which, however, was not surprising because it revealed without possiblity of further doubt, the true motives of a complete campaign of the press, of meetings, of protestations, of rebellions, of schisms, which under the cloak of the defense of the privileges of the Ruthenian Church had already grievously offended against the spirit of reverence and obedience to the Ordinary—even to the extent of depriving him of almost every means of substinence—and weakened the very attachment to the Catholic Faith . . .

Therefore, let every dissension and every suspicion by banished, so that there may be reestablished, in the pride of the common Catholic faith and in fraternal sentiments inspired by a common origin and membership in the same Rite, that mutual charity which should bind closely together all the Ruthenian people in America with their Bishop and clergy, and make of them, even in that land far distant from their native country, a magnificent appeal to dissidents to return to the unity of the Catholic faith.

Your Excellency, who by reason of long practice of office and of affection, has closely at heart the spiritual welfare of the Ruthenian people in the United States, will convey to all the good people, and first of all to Bishop Takach—so sorely and unjustly tried—the trustful word of the Holy Father, who, the guardian of ecclesiastical discipline by reasons of his apostolic ministry, desires that the exact observance of whatever regulations this Sacred Congregation has issued be, on the part of the Ruthenian Church in the United States of America, the most worthy proof of its Catholic faith and of its willingness to live, increase and flourish in works of holiness.

May there descend upon Bishop Takach, his clergy, his faithful— and among them, upon also those who are sorry for their transgressions and return to the proper disposition, the comforting and vivifying blessing of Almighty God, which the Holy Father, through the intercession of the most glorious Virgin Mother, invokes generously and with a fervent prayer that it may be abundant in heavenly graces.

With sentiments of esteem and best wishes, I remain,

Sincerely yours in Christ,
Luigi Cardinal Sincero
Bishop of Palestrina, Sicily
G. Cesarini, Assessor

This letter speaks for itself and it is necessary for me to add only these few words. The letter contains the final word of the Holy See on the matter of celibacy. It is no longer a debatable question. The Holy Father has spoken finally and decisively, and it only remains for us to obey promptly and willingly, as becomes true sons of Holy Mother Church. I am certain that the Holy Father's trust in us is not misplaced.

I am communicating the contents of the letter of the Holy See only to the clergy of the diocese, and it is not to be made known to the laity. The faithful have ever followed with docility the leadership of their priests. If the clergy of the diocese submit humbly, obediently and promptly to this final word of the Holy See, as I am confident they will, there is not doubt but that our faithful people will follow their good example. It is not necessary for me to emphasize the grave responsibility that rests upon you, my dear fathers. The souls of the people are in your hands. Having heard the final word of the Holy See, accept it humbly and obediently; and in a spirit of filial loyalty and devotion to the Supreme Pontiff of Christendom, and like other Christs, as you are by the reason of your sacerdotal powers, continue the work of sanctification and salvation to which you have been called by God for the spiritual welfare and eternal salvation of the Ruthenian people in this country.

My dear Fathers! Like the Vicar of Christ, I too repose full confidence in you. I am certain that the agitation which unfortunately has done so much harm in our diocese will now end. In this confidence and certainty, I bring this communication to a close, praying that each one of you may realize in the fullest measure the blessing which the Holy Father has invoked upon you.

Homestead, Pa.
October 25, 1934
Your benevolent Father in Christ,
†Basil, Bishop

Needless to say the entire text of the response was handed over to the *ARV* by a priest who was incensed by its contents. It was printed in the November 15, 1934 issues of the *ARV*.

The document reveals the utter bewilderment of the Vatican at the situation in the Pittsburgh Greek Catholic Eparchy. The Vatican could not understand why there was a problem with the celibacy issue; after all the married clergy living in the United States were not being disturbed or ordered to return to Europe. Nothing else was being altered in the Greek Catholic Rite, it was only a matter of discipline in the United States. The privilege of a married clergy was still being kept in Europe. The condescension of the Roman See to the Greek Catholic Church is revealed in these words:

"This regulation (celibacy for American clergy) arose,

not new, but anew from the peculiar conditions of the Ruthenian population in the United States of America. There it represents an immigrant element and a minority, and it could not therefore pretend to maintain there its own customs and traditions which are in contrast with those which are the legitimate customs and traditions of Catholicism in the United States, and much less to have there a clergy which could be a source of painful perplexity or scandal to the majority of American Catholics.'

The Vatican saw the problem not in celibacy but in the KOVO National Religious Congress, which it described as "a meeting of intents and manifestations clearly schismatic." The real motive according to the Vatican was not the defense of the Eastern Rite Church but grounds for schism from the Catholic Church.

Bishop Takach's added comments urged the priests to accept the "final word" of the Roman See: "The Holy Father has spoken finally and decisively, and it only remains for us to obey promptly and willingly. . . ." However, Bishop Takach's hope expressed in the letter that the conflict would now end was not to be realized.

The ARV is Placed on the "Index"

In February of 1935, Fr. Stephen Varzaly, who in October of 1933 was reconciled with Bishop Takach and released from excommunication, was suspended once more and excommunicated for his articles in the *ARV* attacking the Roman Catholic Church, the Roman curia and even the Pope. The GCU in September of that year sought to foreclose the mortage on the bishop's residence which it held.[82] (In fact it was only with financial help from the Roman Catholic Diocese of Pittsburgh and a loan from the United Societies that the cathedral itself was saved from sheriff's sale.)

Bishop Takach responded by placing the *ARV* on the

"Index" of literature forbidden to be read by Catholics, on the grounds that is was promoting "religious anarchy."[83] It was now a mortal sin for a Catholic to read the *ARV*. In addition the following congregation were placed under interdict: Saint John the Baptist of Bridgeport, Saint Michael's of Rankin, Pa., and Saint John the Baptist of Perth Amboy, N.J. These churches were denied the ministry of a valid Greek Catholic priest and the sacraments of the church. (Of course they had all been functioning and continued to do so with priests who had long been suspended and excommunicated by Bishop Takach!)

The Officers of the GCU now found themselves in a difficult position. The *ARV* was the official organ of the Union and now it was a mortal sin to read it. The organization maintained that the fight against celibacy was not a fight against the authority of the bishop but only in defense of the Eastern Rite. In addition, many of the members of the GCU would abide by the ruling of the bishop, even if they disagreed with it. The officers of the GCU knew that for the organization to survive they had to come to terms with the bishop so that he would lift the interdict against the *ARV*.

Fr. Varzaly Ousted

The attacks of Fr. Varzaly, the editor of the *ARV*, had been the source of a great deal of consternation to the bishop and the American representatives of the Vatican. Fr. Stephen Varzaly was the price of having the interdict removed.

On December 26, 1935, Michael Yuhasz Sr., GCU President, informed Fr. Varzaly that he was being dismissed as the editor of the *ARV* on the grounds that he no longer was bonded. Fr. Varzaly was unable to be bonded because neither President Yuhasz nor any other officers of the GCU was willing to sign the required documentation.[84]

92

On February 17, 1936, Bishop Takach lifted the interdict on the *ARV* in a letter to Michael Yuhasz, Sr., noting that his request and conditions had been met (presumably the removal of Fr. Varzaly).[85]

However the following week Fr. Varzaly was ordered reinstated as editor by the Common Pleas Court. Fr. Varzaly had successfully maintained that since a convention of the GCU had elected him as editor only a convention could remove him.[86]

The Final Solution — Organization of a New Greek Catholic Diocese

The reply of Rome to the demands of the KOVO National Religious Congress had been, to say the least, negative and the maneuvering of the officers of the GCU in the dismissal of Fr. Stephen Varzaly left the pro-Latinization forces of Bishop Takach and the "traditionalist" forces being unofficially led by Fr. Orestes Chornock, along with Frs. Varzaly and Molchany, in a deadlock, with possibly some slight advantage gained by Bishop Takach, who had discovered in the affair with the *ARV* interdict that the GCU leadership had several chinks in its armor, although the *ARV* continued to publish against celibacy and Latinization.

It was obvious by the end of 1935 that the Roman Church was not going to reverse its stand, expressed in the 1929 decree "Cum Data Fuerit," nor was Bishop Takach going to be recalled, nor were terms of the Union of Uzhorod going to be in force in the United States. There was only one course of action left to those whose religious identity was "Greek Rite" first and Roman Catholic second: the establishment of a new diocese with leaders faithful to their spiritual heritage, who would not betray it or compromise it.

A New Greek Catholic Diocese Established

As early as July of 1935, thirty-seven parishes passed

93

resolutions calling for another "National Religious Congress" to settle once and for all the issue of "Latinization."[87] Since the Vatican was not going to give an inch on the primary issue of celibacy in the Pittsburgh Exarchate, the anti-celibacy forces believed that the Greek Catholic Church could be saved in America by reorganizing and representing itself for union with the Roman Church strictly under the terms of the Union of Uzhorod. The erosion of the Eastern Rite was taking place in the Pittsburgh Exarchate precisely because the conditions of the Union of Uzhorod were being ignored in America by the Roman curia, the bishop and his advisors. Indeed, the majority of the clergy were too concerned with their image as Roman Catholics first and Greek Catholics second to raise their voices in protest. They too easily accepted the adage "Roma locuta causa finita" in the question of celibacy and Latinization.

On February 4, 1936, the clerical leaders of the "anti-celibacy" forces met in the Ft. Pitt Hotel in Pittsburgh, Pennsylvania. At this meeting, which proceeded largely under the direction of Frs. Orestes Chornock, Peter Molchany and the then suspended *ARV* editor Stephen Varzaly, the foundation for a new Greek Catholic diocese was laid.[88]

This "Sobor" of priests, as it referred to itself, elected Fr. Orestes Chornock to serve as administrator of the new diocese until such time as a bishop could be elected.[89] The priests gathered at this meeting also approved the use of the English language in liturgical services, for the benefit especially of those who did not fully understand the Church Slavonic language.[90] At this "Sobor" each priest present contributed $50.00 to establish a newspaper for the new diocese which was entitled simply *Vistnik (Messenger)* of which Fr. Stephen Varzaly was to be the editor.[91]

Fr. Orestes Accepts Administratorship

Although the priests of the newly organized diocese

94

planned to eventually elect a bishop according to the terms of the Union of Uzhorod, they needed a diocesan administrator at once to manage the affairs of the diocese. Besides there was at the time no suitable candidate for the position of bishop—all of the leaders of the new diocese were married priests, while in the Eastern canonical tradition bishops are drawn from the ranks of the monastics.

For his part, Fr. Orestes accepted the position of administrator with these words: "May it be the Lord's will and your will. I take upon myself this office of administrator for His Holy Eastern Greek Catholic Church, for His Carpatho-Russian (Karpato-Russkij narod) people and by His grace given me, I shall labor for the good of the Church and the Russian faithful (virnikov russkich)."[92]

Fr. Orestes Chornock was the best choice for the position of administrator. He had been involved in the "celibacy struggle" since its beginning and in fact was among its first victims. He had been a dynamic priest for over thirty years, and was well acquainted with the situation of the Greek Catholic Church in America. He had been present at the National Religious Congress of 1933 and his charismatic leadership was recognized by all. He also was not afraid to voice his convictions against the will of the majority as when he signed the letter of Fr. Hanulya which was entered into the minutes of the 1933 National Religious Congress protesting several of the resolutions passed by the majority.[93] He was respected by his friends as well as his enemies; Bishop Takach himself sent representatives to Bridgeport to urge him not to accept the position of administrator of the new diocese, realizing that his leadership would be a strong magnet to pull parishes away from the diocese of Pittsburgh.[94] Fr. Orestes was scheduled to be installed as administrator of the new diocese on March 3, 1936, at his parish on Arctic Street in Bridgeport, which was also to become the diocesan seat, although plans at the time called for the person eventually elected bishop to have his seat in Pittsburgh closer to the heart of the Carpatho-Russian diaspora.[95]

The Vistnik—"Published every Thursday for the Defense of the Eastern Rite in America"

So said the words above the editorial column of the new *Vistnik-Messenger*, whose readers touted it as a "worthy successor to the *Amerikanskij Russkij Viestnik*." Without the editoral services of Fr. Varzaly the newspaper had toned down its anti-Latin stance. This publication did much for the cause of the new diocese, and Fr. Varzaly's fiery articles, despite insinuations that are unacceptable by today's standards, began to force the polarization of the Greek Catholic Church into those for "the Russian Administrator Chornock" and those for the "Latin Bishop Takach." According to the *Vistnik* editor, there was no third path.[96]

The early editions of the *Vistnik* carried articles written in English by Michael Roman, one of the leaders of the American born generation of Carpatho-Russians. In his articles Roman emphasized the "Americanness" of the Greek Catholic Church in the United States, its newly acquired love of democracy, and the rights of the individual, including the right of self-expression. In his first article, published in the first issue of the new paper, Roman discussed "freedom of the press and Bishop Takach." He wrote condemning the placing of the *ARV* on the Index by Bishop Takach as "un-American" and that it was even an abrogation of the constitutional right of "freedom of the press." He defended the then ousted editor of the *ARV*, Fr. Varzaly and his "pro-Eastern Rite" articles.[97] Michael Roman's articles helped to keep both the younger generation involved in the struggle and also presented "the case" of the leaders of the new diocese to the English-speaking public at large.

In its anti-Roman articles, the *Vistnik* also began preparing the way for a movement from an "Independent

Greek Catholic Diocese" to a return to the Orthodox Church. However, at this early stage the new diocese was an attempt to reform the Greek Catholic Church in America according to the principles of the Union of Uzhorod to preserve it from a gross Latinization.

Installation of Fr. Administrator Orestes Chornock

On March 3, 1936, at the Bridgeport Church and over the attempts of Bishop Takach to dissuade him, Fr. Orestes Chornock was installed as the administrator of the "Carpatho-Russian Greek Catholic Diocese of the Eastern Rite of the United States in North America,"[98] in a ceremony attended by many priests and faithful who were hoping that this at last would bring peace to the American Greek Catholic Church without compromise. *The Bridgeport Post*, in its edition for Thursday, March 3, 1936, noted that the installation of Fr. Orestes as administrator was to be a temporary position, until a bishop could be elected at a church congress scheduled according to the article "about a year from now."[99]

Bishop Takach did not shrug off the installation. In a letter to the *Bridgeport Times-Star* he condemned it as the work of deposed and schismatic priests and stated that Fr. Chornock had no status in the Greek Catholic Church. Fr. Orestes responded to Bishop Takach's letter by calling it "a pack of lies." Furthermore he stated in an interview with the paper that: "We have been in constant communication with the Holy See of the Roman Catholic Church through Most Rev. Amleto Cicognani, papal nuncio to the United States, seeking the approbation of the church. The group of priests and laity dissenting with Bishop Takach has no intention of breaking away from Rome. We are seeking merely a union with the church that will recognize the right of celibacy and allied privileges granted to the Greek Church in 1646 under the Treaty of Ungvar(Uzhorod) by the Holy See."[100]

The efforts on the part of Fr. Orestes Chornock and of

the leaders of the new diocese to effect some union with the Roman Church were doomed to end in failure. The papal nuncio sought only to have Fr. Orestes return to the fold of the Roman Church with the hope that leaderless the new diocese would crumble.[101] In April 1936, the nuncio informed Bishop Takach that Fr. Orestes Chornock was not in communion with the Roman See.[102] Bishop Takach still attempted to convince Fr. Orestes to return to the Roman Church. In a letter addressed to Bishop Takach of May 5, 1936, Fr. Orestes informed the bishop that he did not need to be reconciled to the church since he was a most faithful member of it and that he would be reconciled with Bishop Takach but only on the condition that the "unfortunate decree "Cum Data Fuerit" be withdrawn and the American Catholic Church recognize the Union of Uzhorod.[103]

Fr. Orestes was retried by the Tribunal of the Pittsburgh Diocese and his sentence of excommunication was allowed to stand. The grounds of his trial was his acceptance of the post of "Administrator of the Carpatho-Russian Greek Catholic Diocese." For all intents and purposes, Fr. Orestes Chornock was the administrator of an independent Greek Catholic Church.

The GCU Convention of 1936

Despite the fact that the new diocese had no canonical recognition from either the Catholic Church or the Orthodox, it attracted a great many Greek Catholics who saw their spiritual tradition being compromised through Latinization. The first test of popular acceptance of the new diocese came at the end of June 1936, at the 22nd GCU Convention held in Wilkes-Barre, Pennsylvania.

Since the ousting of Fr. Varzaly as editor of the *ARV* (though legally reinstated, he was still not functioning), the GCU had begun to move towards reconciliation with the bishop on the matter of celibacy, responding to a loss in membership and pressure from the state of Penn-

98

sylvania's Insurance Board's watchful eye over the GCU activities. When Fr. Administrator Orostes Chornock, Fr. Stephen Varzaly, Fr. Peter Molchany, and many other of the "schismatic and/or excommunicated priests" of the new diocese showed up along with representatives from many parishes under the interdict of Bishop Takach, the credentials committee refused to admit them. The start of the convention was delayed for several days as the sixty-six delegates denied admission took the credentials committee to court. The credentials committee held that only members of the "Greek Catholic Church of the Eastern Rite united with Rome" could be admitted as delegates under the by-laws of the GCU. Since many of the priests denied admission (such as Chornock, Varzaly, and Molchany) had been excommunicated and many of the lay representatives were from congregations that were under interdict of Bishop Takach or had become Russian Orthodox the credentials committee argued that they could not be seated. On the other side, those seeking admission brought out that at the 1930 convention the GCU had adopted an amendment to the by-laws stating: "If the Church Authority should suspend or excommunicate or punish in any manner any member as a result of his activity in defending the rights, privileges, traditions and discipline of our Eastern Rite Greek Catholic Church, acting in the sense and under the conditions of the contract of Union 1646 in Uzhorod, such action on the part of the Church Authority cannot be the cause for depriving anybody of his office in the Greek Catholic Union of Russian Brotherhoods nor of his membership in said organization."[104] They further charged that the existing officers of the GCU felt that their chances of being re-elected were better without the barred delegates being admitted.

At this point the Pennsylvania Insurance Department stepped in acting on a complaint from an anonymous delegate that the start of the convention was being delayed and that this was costing the GCU thousands of dollars, far more than the budget of the convention. (The delegates were paid $6.00 per day for attending the sessions for expenses.) The Insurance Department kept a close watch on the GCU since it had tottered on financial disaster in 1930. State investigators were dispatched and fixed the blame on the officers of the GCU. Addressing the assembled delegates, investigator David Roache impressed upon them the need to "get down to business" and to keep costs down, even though he pointed out that the organization was perfectly solvent and one of the wealthiest of its size in the state.[105]

In the end forty-five of the sixty-six delegates were seated, as well as Frs. Orestes Chornock, Stephen Varzaly, Peter Molchany, and a fourth priest excommunicated for his anti-celibacy activity, Constantine Auroroff. These priests were seated by a vote of the delegates (197 to 140).[106]

Although this vote reveals the growing split in the GCU between those supporting Bishop Takach and the "anti-Latinization" group of which Fr. Orestes Chornock was administrator, Fr. Stephen Varzaly was elected to edit the *ARV* newspaper and, further, Fr. Peter Molchany was chosen to be the spiritual advisor of the GCU. In addition, George Ferrio, an attorney from the Bridgeport parish and supporter of Fr. Chornock, was chosen to replace George L. Puhak, a supporter of Bishop Takach, as legal advisor of the GCU.[107]

Elected as president of the GCU in 1936 was John Sekerak whose platform included working for the defence of the Eastern Rite, and one of his first acts was to address Bishop Takach, asking for peace in the diocese and the recall of "Cum Data Fuerit" and printed in the *ARV* on July 8, 1937.

Despite these seeming victories for the "anti-Latinization" faction for the control of the GCU, shortly after the Wilkes-Barre Convention the organization began to lean more and more towards reconciliation with the bishop. There were several reasons for this. First of all, as the result of the Wilkes-Barre Convention, by a vote of 409 in favor and 105 opposed the GCU delegates, both the Sokol (Junior) and regular members amended the charter of the organization to eliminate its ties with any church (although when asked at least one of the officers said, "this does not mean however that we will not continue to recognize the Pope of Rome").[108] This sentiment was partially the result of the pressure exerted upon the convention by the Pennsylvania Insurance Department to conduct an orderly convention without the "religious question" as a cause of debate, since this had nothing to do with fraternal insurance (in the Department's view anyway). The end result of this was that the way was paved for the GCU to take a more neutral position in the controversy, which was beginning to cost it both members and money. Michael Roman, who originally had written for the *Vistnik* against celibacy, became one of the spokesmen for this position of "peace" for the good of the organization, the church and people.[109] Roman had been elected editor of the *Sokol,* the GCU organ for the junior Sokol branch of the organization at the Wilkes-Barre Convention and would eventually become the editor of the *ARV.*

Another reason for the GCU willingness to compromise with the bishop was the fact that the KOVO efforts to end celibacy had failed, and the new "diocese," of which Fr. Orestes Chornock was administrator, did not receive any support from the Roman authorities. The GCU had, since the start of the fight against celibacy, maintained that it was not fighting against the authority of the pope, despite the resolutions of the 1933 National Religious Congress. The organization was now in the awkward position of having to choose between Bishop Takach and Fr. Orestes Chornock. For the moment though it appeared after the 1936 Convention that Fr. Administrator Orestes Chornock and the "Carpatho-Russian Greek Catholic Diocese of the

Eastern Rite" had a great deal of support in the GCU.

Response of the Vatican

In a letter dated October 29, 1936 and made public by its recipient, Bishop Takach, on November 29 of the same year, the Vatican gave its final ruling in regards to any recognition the "Carpatho-Russian Greek Catholic Diocese of the Eastern Rite" may have sought to gain from it. The Vatican viewed it as nothing more than a "schismatic movement" whose leaders were "wolves in sheep's clothing" and the pope himself pronounced as excommunicated "nominatum" the following priests because of their association with the "schismatic" movement: Orestes Chornock, Stephen Varzaly, Constantine Auroroff, Irenaeus Dolhy, Peter Molchany, and John Soroka. The Pope also condemned this new diocese and "every writing which supported the schismatic movement headed by Orestes Chornock."[110]

For their part the leaders of the "Carpatho-Russian Greek Catholic Diocese" had in fact already declared themselves "independent of Rome" publicly almost two weeks before their excommunication by Pope Pius XI on October 17, 1936. The charge has been made that Fr. Orestes Chornock used "the role of a Greek Catholic priest in communion with Rome but against celibacy and in favor of the privileges of the Union of Uzhorod" to win people to his new church. Yet the new diocese only came into existence in February of 1936. Before this, Fr. Orestes and the other priests excommunicated by Bishop Takach did not deny their excommunication by him, nor was it any secret to anyone who in the very least was interested in the affairs of the Greek Catholic Church. Fr. Orestes and the others, both clerical and lay, regarded these excommunications as the work of a frustrated bishop and believed that when celibacy had been recalled these excommunications would be as well. By the end of 1935, Fr. Orestes Chornock and the other leaders of the new diocese saw that Bishop Takach and celibacy were not going to be recalled, and that the Pittsburgh diocese was leaning more and more to the example of the Latin Rite Church. Bishop Takach himself introduced such devotions, alien to the Greek Catholic Church, as the Sacred Heart, the Stations of the Cross, and the Novena, using texts that for the most part were translated from Latin into Church Slavonic. In forming the "Carpatho-Russian Greek Catholic Diocese" Fr. Orestes Chornock and the other leaders of the "anti-Latinization" struggle were seeking to establish a Greek Catholic Church whose spiritual heritage would be recognized by Rome without question or threat of "Latinization," as Fr. Orestes stated to the Bridgeport *Times-Star* at the time of his installation as administrator.

By the summer of 1936, it became apparent to all that, apart from attempts to induce Fr. Orestes to step down as administrator, Rome was not going to enter into any sort of "union" with the Carpatho-Russian Greek Catholic Diocese, especially given the anti-Roman bias of the *Vistnik* under the editorship of Fr. Varzaly.

On October 1, 1936, the *Vistnik* carried a statement on its front page written in response to an article in *Prosvita* declaring: "Yes, We are Independent."[111] The article went on to state that the new diocese was "independent of the Italian agent Takach." It continued to declare that "we do not live in Hungary under the authority of the Hungarian gendarmes nor under the power of the Italian (Pope) . . . We only worship God and are only obligated to the laws of America and no other! . . . We are Russian Americans (*russkimi Amerikancami*), who love our Eastern Rite and America, our new Fatherland, where we live . . ."[112]

The Vatican's excommunications of the leaders of the "Carpatho-Russian Greek Catholic Diocese" came on October 17, 1936, although it was not until the end of November that the clergy and faithful of the Pittsburgh Greek Catholic Diocese were made aware of them by

Bishop Takach. In any case, the die had been cast. For Fr. Orestes Chornock, for the other priests of the Carpatho-Russian Greek Catholic Diocese, the churches, and faithful who had become members of it, there was no longer any possibility of returning to the Roman Church and maintaining their spiritual tradition in it.

1937 — The Stones Are Cast Away

The beginning of the year 1937 saw many of the parishes of the "new Greek Catholic Diocese" under Administrator Orestes Chornock embroiled in court battles between the "Independents" (as the followers of Fr. Orestes were called) and the followers of Bishop Takach. Even the seat of the new diocese, the parish of Fr. Orestes, Saint John the Baptist on Arctic Street in Bridgeport was involved in lengthy court litigation. In some cases, such as Saint Nicholas of Homestead, where Fr. Molchany was the pastor, new churches were being built, as the old buildings were awarded to the "Uniates."

The history of these court cases is complex and lengthy and the confusion and lack of uniformity in the chartering of churches originally makes each case almost unique. In the case of the Bridgeport parish, it was not Bishop Takach who brought suit, but the Roman Catholic bishop of Hartford, to whom the parishioners had gone decades earlier to secure authorization for the building of their church. The suit was begun in 1932, at almost the start of the struggle and was not resolved completely until 1944.

Early in 1937, *Vostok* the newspaper of the fraternal organization "Svoboda-Liberty," bore the news that the Perth Amboy parish's charter amendments made in 1924, incorporating the parish property into the Pittsburgh Greek Catholic Diocese were declared illegal by the court and the parish was free to join the "independent Russian Greek Catholic Diocese" of Fr. Administrator Orestes Chornock. It is no surprise that the Liberty Organization, through its close association with the Perth Amboy parish, gave gavo complete support to Fr. Chornock, just as the parish did. Those in Perth Amboy who sought to remain loyal to the Uniate (as the "Independents" were calling it now) Church, were forced to hold services in a nearby Catholic school and to eventually build a new church. Fr. Administrator Orestes Chornock assigned one of the priests, recently excommunicated by the Pope with him as the pastor—Fr. Irenaeus Dolhy, a staunch defender of the Eastern spiritual tradition.

In the closing months of 1936 and in the beginning of 1937, the articles in the *Vistnik* began to take a new tact, not only was there found polemic against Bishop Takach and Latinization, but the papal primacy of jurisdiction and the primacy of the Roman Church itself was questioned.

The "Eastern nature" of the early Church was discussed with the conclusion that the "true" faith lay elsewhere than the Vatican. It lay in the Orthodox Church, the Church which was the heir to the spiritual tradition of the ancient Church Fathers and Councils. It became more and more obvious that the "Carpatho-Russian Greek Catholic Diocese of the Eastern Rite" was moving farther away from its earlier expressed desire for Union with Rome according to the "terms of the Union of Uzhorod" to embacing the Orthodox faith once more, as its ancestors had three centuries earlier.

In the late 1890s and the early decades of the twentieth century, Greek Catholic polemicists denounced Orthodoxy as "the faith of Toth" and Orthodox Christians as "schismatics." Exaggerated stories appeared in the *ARV* telling of how (in the days before the Russian revolution), hundreds of thousands of rubles were poured into the American Mission of the Russian Orthodox Church to entice Greek Catholic priests and churches to join it. (The letters of Fr. Toth reveal that he was frequently short of funds!)[113]

Many Greek Catholic parishes, particularly those that were Gallician, did in fact identify with the Russian

Orthodox Church, particularly in resisting attempts to make them "Ukrainian." These parishes formed for the most part the bulk of the "Russian Orthodox Church" in the Eastern United States. However many of these Orthodox parishes, especially after the Russian Revolution when all funding was cut off, were rather poor in comparison with the "Greek Catholic" Church, and there existed an enmity between the "Russian Orthodox Greek Catholics" and the "Russian Greek Catholics United with Rome."

The "Karpato-Russkij Sojuz"

Ironically, this wall of enmity began to crumble at the National Religious Congress of 1933, when the "Karpato-Russkij Sojuz" (The Carpatho-Russian Union) was established to promote cultural, social, and political affairs among Carpatho-Russians, Orthodox, and Uniate alike.[114] Through the Sojuz the Uniates were able to glimpse church life among the Orthodox and to foster their understanding of the Orthodox faith. A symphonic choir was established under the direction of Fr. Michael Tidick, an Orthodox priest and Fr. Michael Staurovsky, a Uniate.[115]

Most of the Carpatho-Russian Orthodox were former Uniates themselves and usually called themselves "Russian Orthodox Greek Catholics." The largest Russian Orthodox Church in the United States, before changing its name to the "Orthodox Church in America" in 1970, was known officially as the "Russian Orthodox Greek Catholic Church of America.[116]

As a result of court cases between Orthodox, or "Independents" and the Greek Catholic Diocese of Pittsburgh, the term "Greek Catholic" was no longer interpreted in America as meaning "Eastern Rite united with Rome" but was simply taken to be a generic term for anyone who followed the "Greek Rite" in worship: Orthodox, "Independent," or Catholic. (This is not true in Europe however, where "Greek Catholic" means "united with Rome.") As a result of this, the members of the Pittsburgh diocese were encouraged to call themselves "Catholics of the Byzantine-Slavonic Rite" or simply "Byzantine-Rite Catholics," to emphasize their commitment to the Roman Church. The word Orthodox (pravoslavnyj) was replaced in their services with "true-believing" (pravovirnyj).[117] This change of terms gave further credence to the charge that Bishop Takach was in fact altering the "Faith."

In the midst of all this, Fr. Administrator Orestes Chornock also came to realize, with the rest of the leaders of the new diocese, that they could not continue to exist as an "independent church." They were painfully aware that an "independent church" was independent from both apostolic tradition and succession, independent from an authentic spiritual life, independent from the communion of the Holy Spirit, the fountain of the very life of the Church itself. Fr. Orestes Chornock was not an anarchist; it was the violation of what he saw as his legal rights as a member of the Greek Catholic Church united with Rome under the Union of Uzhorod that roused him to protest the introduction of celibacy and Latinization.

The fact that the new diocese had no bishop and no canonical standing also weighed heavily on Fr. Orestes. The bishop in the Eastern tradition he loved so well was the person who authenticated the life of the Church; no Liturgy could be served without the bishop's blessing given through the antimension; no priests could be ordained and the new diocese was desperately short of trained and qualified priests. If the new diocese was to be more than a loose confederation of "independent" dissident Greek Catholic parishes, if it was ever to live and grow in the Eastern spiritual tradition, if it ever was to stand united, it would have to have a worthy "Father in Christ," a canonical bishop to lead it. For the time being there was no such person on the horizon and Fr. Orestes, as the administrator of the diocese was forced to cope as best he could with these trying and difficult situations, accepting priests from the Russian Orthodox. A few candidates were ordained by the "Orthodox" Carpatho-Russian Bishop Adam Philipovsky. The majority of the priests of the new diocese were, like the Fr. Administrator, former priests of the Pittsburgh Greek Catholic diocese who were either excommunicated or simply chose to leave on account of their resistance to Bishop Takach's enforcement of the "Cum Data Fuerit" decree.

For the part, in making known the October 1936 excommunication of the leaders of the new diocese, Bishop Takach ordered prayers to be said "for the reform of the wayward" during the Advent season, a Paraklis' to the Mother of God or an Acathist to the Sacred Heart.[118]

Another event occurred in 1937 that was to have a great effect of the life of Fr. Orestes Chornock. His beloved "Pani" Yolanda passed away on May 28, 1937 at the age of fifty-two. Described by the parishioners of her husband's parish as a "great and generous lady," she had given him her support through the dark times of the early 1930s. It was at this trying position of "Fr. Administrator" that he needed her support and counsel the most and he felt her loss keenly.

As the year progressed there came renewed calls for another "National Religious Congress" with the participation of lay delegates and cantors from each of the parishes who placed themselves in the "Independent" diocese as well as for participation from delegates of parishes still in the Pittsburgh diocese legally, but who had large factions in their congregations supportive of Fr. Administrator Orestes Chornock. The date of the Congress was set for Monday, November 22, 1937 at the downtown Pittsburgh Y.M.C.A.

The "National Religious Congress" of 1937

The initial support given to the leaders of the new diocese at the 1936 GCU convention by its delegates began to wane in 1937 among the executive board of the GCU. The President John Sekerak, who had been the candidate favored by those opposed to Bishop Takach soon clashed with Fr. Varzaly, re-elected as *ARV* editor, over administrative matters at the GCU Headquarters in Homestead. This led to Fr. Varzaly being dismissed as the *ARV* editor in September of 1937 by President Sekerak. Michael Roman, who had also been the choice of those opposed to Bishop Takach as *Sokol* editor at the 1936 GCU convention, but who now was advocating reconciliation with the bishop, was elevated to be editor of the *ARV* in place of Fr. Varzaly. Only the dynamic Fr. Molchany, elected as spiritual advisor of the GCU in 1936, remained completely committed to Fr. Orestes Chornock and his new diocese of the GCU officers.

Despite these setbacks in the GCU, the "Congress" called by Fr. Administrator Orestes Chornock opened on Monday at 3:00 p.m. on November 22, 1937, with 135 delegates present representing 46 parishes.[119] The first day of the convention was taken up with strong speeches against the past abuses of the "Eastern Rite" by Rome and recalling that it was from the city of Constantinople that the Carpatho-Russian people received the Orthodox Faith centuries before the "Unia" came into existence. Fr. Stephen Varzaly made an especially long passionate speech, condemning the "haughtiness of Rome" and its desire to see wiped off "the face of the earth the Eastern Church." It was the Eastern Church, he proclaimed, which "kept the faith of Christ and the Apostles with its bishops and faithful." He recalled the work of Saints Cyril and Methodios, the events of 1054 which he attributed to the pride of Rome, the destruction of the Eastern Rite by Rome among the Italo-Greeks, the Hungarians, the Syrians, and the Maronites. He recalled the Unions of 1595 and 1646 among the Galicians and the Carpatho-Russians and denounced them as attempts at "Latinization." He saw in the expression "Graeca fides—nulla fides" the attitude of Rome to the Eastern Churches. He recounted the history of the celibacy struggle in America and the number of legitimate protests sent to Rome concerning it. He went on to remind the delegates that "we did not come here to write letters to Rome or to send delegates to Rome . . . . It is necessary for us to now look to the future and to give strong moral and material strength to the renewal of our diocese." The purpose of the Congress, Fr. Varzaly stated was to build up the church and the diocese and for this work there was need of a "faithful, Russian, Eastern bishop."

Another speaker who had great influence on the first day of the Congress was Fr. Peter Molchany. In his address Fr. Molchany pointed out that Bishop Takach already had removed from the service books the word "Orthodox" that had always been found. Fr. Molchany called himself a member of the "Russian Greek-Catholic Eastern-Rite Church." Bishop Takach, however, now referred to himself as a "Roman Catholic of the Greek Rite." Fr. Molchany pointed out that the Carpatho-Russians first received their faith from Constantinople, where Saint John Chrysostom was patriarch and that today the Patriarch of Constantinople was Orthodox. He reminded the delegates that the "Apostles of the Slavs," Cyril and Methodios, were Greeks and that the word "catholic" itself was a Greek word meaning "universal."

At this point some of the lay delegates expressed concerns over using the term "Orthodox" and abandoning "Greek Catholic," especially since in many cases in disputes over church properties with Bishop Takach the term "Greek Catholic" had become fixed by the courts in many church charters. Fr. Varzaly spoke up saying, "Do not be afraid of the word 'Orthodox' . . . . In spirit and by rights we are Orthodox, but before the courts (because of legal concerns over properties) we must officially call ourselves "Greek Catholic."

As a result of this at the next day of the Congress the delegates chose to call their diocese the "Carpatho-Russian

Greek Catholic Diocese of the Eastern Rite of the U.S.A."

After the vote was taken to approve this name Fr. Irenaeus Dolhy addressed the delegates on the need for a bishop to rule the diocese and to lead it. In his talk he proposed Fr. Administrator Orestes Chornock, who being recently widowed, was now elegible for the hierarchy. Fr. Dolhy placed the record of Fr. Orestes before the delegates, telling them, "The book of Fr. Administrator is open for all Carpatho-Russian Americans."

Upon concluding his remarks, Fr. Dolhy called upon the clergy present to elect a worthy candidate to be bishop of the new diocese. (In accordance with the Union of Uzhorod, which served as the basis for the election, only the clergy delegates could vote; the lay delegates were present as witnesses of the election.) The minutes of the Congress remark that "this was a great and touching moment." A platform was set up, upon which there was an *analogion*. Spread out on the *analogion* was an *aer (vozduch)* and upon that a gold chalice into which each priest would place his ballot containing the name of his choice for bishop. The minutes of the Congress continue:

> With great reverence Fr. Dolhy placed an *epitrachil* upon himself and kneeling with all the clerical and civilian delegates began to sing, 'O Heavenly King,' so that the Holy Spirit would help the priests choose a worthy candidate for the episcopacy. At the end of the prayer, all of the priests came up to the holy chalice and placed their ballots in it. When this ended then Fr. Molchany opened the ballots one by one and read aloud the name written on it. All of the ballots indicated as worthy the name 'The Most Reverend Fr. Administrator Orestes Chornock.' The Fr. Dolhy said: "It is willed by the Holy Spirit and by us to elect as bishop for our new diocese Fr. Chornock." And the priests sang *"Eis polla eti, Despota"* and the people sang *"Many Years."*[120]

The minutes of the Congress recorded that Fr. Orestes accepted reluctantly, and only because he knew that if the diocese was to exist in deed and not just in word it would need a bishop. At this the record of the proceedings states that there were tears in the eyes of the bishop-elect, of the priests and of the lay delegates. Then: "Fr. Dolhy announced with joy that the work was completed . . . 'We have a diocese and we have a candidate for the episcopacy.' "[121]

Much of the third day of the Congress was given over to the discussion of the Carpatho-Russian Sojuz organization. As mentioned earlier, this organization sought to promote the Carpatho-Russian nationality and included both Orthodox and Greek Catholics. The "independent" Carpatho-Russian diocese was in a vulnerable position in this organization. Many of the Russian Orthodox attempted to attract "independents" to the already existing Russian Orthodox dioceses; conversely the Uniate Greek Catholics attempted to lure them back into the fold of the Catholic Church. Especially odious to the "independents" was the person of Fr. Michael Staurovsky, who had been revealed as Bishop Takach's agent in the "administration" of Fr. Orestes Chornock, sending reports to Bishop Takach on all its internal affairs. After his exposure Fr. Staurovsky published a paper titled *Straz (Guardian)* which ridiculed and slandered Fr. Orestes Chornock and the other leaders of the then "independent diocese.[122] Fr. Staurovsky was a leading figure in the Sojuz.

It is no surprise then read in the minutes that the Congress unanimously passed a resolution to grant no recognition to the Carpatho-Russian Sojuz and to condemn it as being "full of traitors to the Eastern church and Carpatho-Russian people."[123]

Also on the third day reports were given regarding the many organizations for the young people that existed on the local level in the parishes. The new Bishop-elect Orestes Chornock was fond of saying that the young people of a parish were its pearls and a parish without many was poor indeed. The delegates passed a resolution to establish a diocesan youth organization that would have chapters in each parish. The Bishop-elect would be the head of the organization which would have its own by-laws and would have a national convention once-a-year at which spiritual and Carpatho-Russian ethnic questions would be discussed. The name of the organization was to be "The Sons and Daughters of the Eastern Church" and it would publish a journal entitled "Carpatho-Russian Youth."[124] The editor was to be Joseph Mihaly of Stratford, Connecticut.

On the third day as well committees were formed to compile a set of statutes for the new diocese. The Congress ended on the third day with Fr. Peter Molchany leading the singing of "Dostojno jest."

"Neither to Rome nor to Moscow"

In electing Fr. Orestes Chornock to be the candidate for the episcopacy of the new diocese, the Congress, which later came to be recognized as the "First Diocesan Sobor," broke all ties with Rome and the Union of Uzhorod. The only question remaining was where would the bishop-elect seek consecration.

In speaking of the history of the church in Karpatska-Rus' at the Congress, the priest-delegates Varzaly and Molchany recounted that it was from Constantinople that the Orthodox brothers Cyril and Methodios brought the faith and that Saint John Chrysostom, whose Liturgy was celebrated most Sundays during the year, had been the Patriarch of Constantinople.

The Orthodox Church in Karpatska Rus' before the Union of Uzhorod had been under the jurisdiction of the Metropolitan of Kiev who, before 1686, was subject to the Ecumenical Patriarchate of Constantinople.

As early as 1932 it had been proposed by a lay member of the KOVO that if the Vatican would not

113

respond to requests for the repeal of "Cum Data Fuerit" a delegation be sent to the Patriarch of Constantinople in Turkey.[125]

Even though the Greek Catholic Church had come into existence in Karpatska-Rus' in 1646, its members still retained memories of their links with the Orthodox Church through Kiev and Constantinople.(Kiev came under the jurisdiction of Moscow in 1686, forty years after the Union of Uzhorod.)

"Nor to Moscow"

The casual observer may often raise the question as to why the "independent" Greek Catholic Diocese did not join the existing Russian Orthodox Church as had Fr. Toth and many Carpatho-Russian Greek Catholic parishes done at the turn of the century.

One author of the former Russian Orthodox Greek Catholic Church (Metropolia), now called the Orthodox Church in America, asserts that Fr. Orestes' and the other leaders of the diocese turn to Constantinople and not to one of the existing Russian dioceses in America was motivated by "the desire of the groups leaders to have the highest ecclesiastical sanction of the Orthodox Church as they understood it, and also to be free to practice their uniquely Carpatho-Russian customs and traditions as they had desired in their break from Rome." In fact talks had been held between the leaders of the new diocese and representatives of the Russian American "Metropolia" but they yielded no fruit.

Orthodoxy in America in the Early 20th Century

When Fr. Toth lead the first return of Carpatho-Russian immigrants to the Orthodox Faith in 1891 until his death in 1909 an estimated 25,000 Carpatho-Russians, most of whom were Galicians, returned to the Orthodox Church.[126]

At this time there existed only one Orthodox jurisdiction in the United States, the Russian Orthodox Diocese of Alaska and the Aleutians, whose bishop resided in San Francisco. In the course of Fr. Toth's career, especially as a result of his career, the number of Orthodox parishes in the Eastern United States, composed of former "Uniates," would alter the name of the diocese to that of "the Aleutians and North America" and see a change in the diocesan seat as well.[127]

The diocese of the Aleutians and North America showed great promise under the far-sighted administration of Bishop Tikhon (later Patriarch); his return to Russia in 1907 was without a doubt a setback to nascent American Orthodoxy and in the following years, especially after World War I, there was a greater emphasis placed on ethnic culture among the Orthodox, leading to the establishment of separate Russian, Greek, Serbian, Antiochene, and several other "ethnic" jurisdictions. The Russian Church in America was split into three groups: the Russian Orthodox Greek Catholic Church, known also as the "Metropolia" (since 1970—the Orthodox Church in America), which sought to remain loyal to the Russian Church in Russia, however insisting on its own autonomy and refusing loyalty to the Soviet government; the Russian Orthodox Church Outside of Russia, which refused to recognize the Patriarchate under Soviet domination; and lastly the Exarchate of the Patriarch of Moscow (the Russian Orthodox Church in the U.S.A.), consisting of those parishes and clergy which unlike the other groups remained directly under the authority of the Patriarch of Moscow.

There had been an attempt made by the Russian Orthodox to set up a separate diocese for "Carpatho-Russians" in the waning days of the Russian Mission and the "North American Diocese" with its own bishop, a former Greek Catholic priest named Alexander Dzubay.

Bishop Stephen Dzubay

Alexander Dzubay was not simply a parish priest in the Greek Catholic Church. Active in America since 1889, he was one of the "pioneer" Greek Catholic priests and was instrumental in the founding and development of many Greek Catholic churches. Respect for him was so great by 1913 that his fellow priests elected him as vicar-general under Bishop Soter Ortinsky.

Upon the death of Bishop Ortinsky in 1916, Fr. Alexander Dzubay, as the senior priest of the diocese, as a widower and with the full support of the Greek Catholic Union, had expectations of becoming the next bishop, or at least apostolic administrator for the "Ruthenians" as Rome called Carpatho-Russians. Instead he was passed over by the Vatican and Gabriel Martyak became "Ruthenian" administrator.

Bitterly disappointed, he left the Greek Catholic diocese and in short order (from July 30 to August 7, 1916) was consecrated as an Orthodox bishop by the Russian bishops Evdokim, Alexander, and Metropolitan Herman at Saint Nicholas Cathedral in New York City, taking the name he chose as a monastic, "Stephen."[128] Bishop Stephen Dzubay's task was to head a Carpatho-Russian "subdiocese of Pittsburgh" that would exist solely for re-uniting Uniate Carpatho-Russians with the Orthodox Church. Unfortunately, Bishop Stephen's "Carpatho-Russian" diocese of Pittsburgh was never permitted to formally exist. Bishop Stephen himself was active in consecrating several churches but was denied jurisdiction by the "Great Russian" bishops, who incorporated the parishes into their respective flocks.[129]

Frustrated by being relegated to the role of a "second-class" hierarch, Bishop Stephen took advantage of the disruption of church order in America that came upon the heels of the Russian Revolution. On October 26, 1922, acting as the self-proclaimed "acting head" of the diocese of North America, a position he felt was in keeping with his being the senior bishop of the diocese at the time, he consecrated as "Bishop of Canada" another Carpatho-Russian, Adam Philipovsky, though the canonical circumstances of the consecration were held to be questionable.[130]

On November 25-27, 1922, the All-American Sobor of the diocese elected Metropolitan Platon as its head. He received confirmation from Patriarch of Moscow Tikhon. On December 5, 1922, Bishop Stephen convened a "counter-Sobor," challenging the authenticity of Platon's patriarchal confirmation and claiming that as senior auxiliary bishop he was by right the legal "acting" ruling bishop of the diocese. Bishop Stephen brought legal suit against Metropolitan Platon to prevent him from functioning as the head of the diocese.

Although initially supported by several priests and Bishop Adam, in 1923, Bishop Stephen withdrew his legal challenge and, making peace with Metropolitan Platon, was accepted again as senior auxiliary bishop of the diocese. In 1924, frustrated by his dealings with the "Great Russian" administration of the diocese, and bitter at his failed attempt for personal recognition and authority, Bishop Stephen renounced the Orthodox faith and returned to the Uniate Church, spending the last years of his life in penance at the Roman Catholic Franciscan Monastery in Graymoor, New York.

Bishop Adam became the leader of an "independent" group of Carpatho-Russian parishes (some forty churches). In 1935 he rejoined the then "Russian Orthodox Greek Catholic Church" and one by one his parishes were absorbed by the "Great Russian" hierarchy into their territories. Even though the bulk of the "Metropolia" consisted of Carpatho-Russian immigrants its hierarchy, for the most part of "Great Russian" background, would not consent to a separate Carpatho-Russian diocese or jurisdiction within the framework of their church. In 1943, Bishop Adam left the "Metropolia" and joined the Russian "Patriarchal"

117

jurisdiction under its Exarch, Benjamin.[131]

The examples of Bishop Stephen and Bishop Adam made most Carpatho-Russians skeptical about becoming members of the "Russian Orthodox Greek Catholic Church." Those Carpatho-Russians who had joined it gradually lost their spiritual tradition and became totally "Russified." Great Russian priests and hierarchs referred to Carpatho-Russians as *Parchato-Russy* (uncouth Russians!). Carpatho-Russian *prostopinije* (congregational singing) was cacaphonic "Latinization" to the ears of clergy used to Russian choral singing and for the most part was systematically destroyed, even though the noted Orthodox chant scholar, Johann von Gardner, wrote that it was only in Carpatho-Russia, through the *prostopinije,* that he heard chanting according to the directives of the Church Typicon.[132]

To be sure there were "Latinizations" in the Uniate Greek Catholic Church, such as First Holy Communion, the benediction of the Blessed Sacrament, and several liturgical externals approved at the Synod of Zamosc.[133] However, many of the so-called "Latinizations" of the Carpatho-Russian Greek Catholics were elements that Patriarch Nicon had purged from the Russian Church in the mid-seventeenth century in his "reformation" of the church. Carpatho-Russians still used the pre-Niconian Slavonic text for their services and on the whole their Typicon presented a mixture of Greek, Russian and Russian Old Believer elements when purged of any "Latinizations." The "Union" of 1646 cut off the Carpatho-Russians from the "reforms" of Nicon. With a typically "Byzantine" chauvinism these distinct elements were eliminated by the Great Russians as all being "Latin."

With all of this in mind, the leaders of the new diocese, Fr. Orestes Chornock, Frs. Varzaly and Molchany, and the others, did not want to escape the threat of "Latinization" only to be threatened by "Russification." In order to safeguard their Carpatho-Russian spiritual tradition they insisted that Fr. Orestes had to be consecrated as the bishop of their diocese with full jurisdiction. The spokesmen for the "Metropolia" felt that there was no need of another "Carpatho-Russian" bishop in the church, citing the existence of Bishop Adam, who had ordained already several priests for the new diocese.[134] These terms were not acceptable to Fr. Orestes and the other priests of the diocese. Fr. Molchany, who had been an early advocate of a return to the jurisdiction of the Ecumenical Patriarchate of Constantinople, was sent to New York to meet with the Exarch of the Ecumenical Patriarch, Athenagoras (later Patriarch himself), to discuss the possibility of the new diocese being under the Patriarch's jurisdiction and the consecration of Fr. Orestes Chornock as its bishop.[135]

Through the office of Archbishop Athenagoras, the minutes of the November 1937 "Sobor" at which the Unia was abrogated and Fr. Orestes elected to be the episcopal candidate were forwarded to the Synod of the Ecumenical Patriarchate, along with a memorandum outlining the liturgical life of the Carpatho-Russian Church.[136] Archbishop Athenagoras greatly interested himself in the cause of the new diocese and would later refer to himself as its "godfather."

Fr. Orestes Consecrated as Titualar Bishop of Agathonikeia

Encouraged by the acceptance of former Ukrainian Uniates by the Patriarch and the consecration of the Rev. Dr. Joseph Zuk as their bishop several years earlier (in August of 1932), Fr. Orestes, the priests and the faithful of the diocese began to look forward to the day when they would be Orthodox again, just as their ancestors were and free to practice their faith without the approval of Rome.

In the summer of 1938 word was finally received. The Patriarch, Benjamin I, and the Holy Synod would accept the Carpatho-Russians and allow them to preserve their ecclesiastical integrity. On August 24, 1938, Bishop-elect Orestes Chornock, Fr. Joseph Mihaly (who had been previously ordained by Archbishop Athenagoras), and a lay representative, John Onofrey, boarded ship for Constantinople. On September 18, 1938, he was consecrated in the Patriarchal Cathedral of Saint George the Trophy-Bearer by three metropolitan members of the Holy Synod: Germanos of Sardis and Pisidia, Constantine of Eirenopolis, and Dorotheos of Laodicaea. Bishop Orestes was elected as bishop of the titular see of Agathonikeia, an ancient see of the Patriarchate whose name meant fittingly, "Good Victory." He had been canonically elected by the Holy Synod of the Patriarchate two days before his consecration on September 16, 1938. On September 19, 1938, the "Carpatho-Russian Greek Catholic Diocese of the Eastern Rite of the U.S.A." was canonized as a diocese of the Ecumenical Patriarchate by Patriarch Benjamin I in patriarchal decree 1379:[137]

Patriarchal Synod's Document of Consecration of The Most Reverend Bishop Orestes.
Dokument Patriaršoho Synoda o Chirotoniji Preosvjasčenňijšoho Episkopa Oresta.

'Αδεία καὶ προτροπῇ τῆς αὐτοῦ θειοτάτης Παναγιότητος τοῦ Οἰκουμενικοῦ Πατριέρχου Βενιαμὶν Α΄, ἡμεῖς οἱ ὑποσημειούμενοι μητροπολῖται Σάρδεων καὶ Πισιδίας Γερμανός,Εἰρηνουπόλεως Κωνσταντῖνος καὶ Λαοδικείας Δωρόθεος,μέλη τῆς Ἁγίας καὶ Ἱερᾶς Πατριαρχικῆς Συνόδου τοῦ Οἰκουμενικοῦ Θρόνου,Ἱ-ερουργήσαντες σήμερον Κυριακήν,δεκάτην ὀγδόην μηνὸς Σεπτεμβρίου τοῦ χιλιοστοῦ ἐννεακοσιοστοῦ τρι ακοστοῦ ὀγδόου σωτηρίου ἔτους,ἐν τῷ Πανσέπτῳ Πατριαρχικῷ Ναῷ τοῦ Ἁγίου Ἐνδόξου Μεγαλομάρτυρος Γεωργίου τοῦ Τροπαιοφόρου,κεχειροτονήκαμεν εἰς Ἐπίσκοπον,τῇ χάριτι τοῦ Παναγίου καὶ Τελεταρχι-κοῦ Πνεύματος,τὸν διὰ ψήφων κανονικῶν τῆς Ἁγίας καὶ Ἱερᾶς Πατριαρχικῆς Συνόδου,ἐπὶ ψιλῷ ὀνόματι τῆς πάλαι ποτὲ διαλαμψάσης Ἁγιωτάτης Ἐπισκοπῆς Ἁγαθονικείας εἰς τὸ ἐπισκοπικὸν Ἀξίωμα ἀναχθέντα αἰδεσιμολογιώτατον ἐν πρεσβυτέροις Ὀρέστην Τσορνόκ,ἐκ τῶν κληρικῶν τῶν ἐν Ἀμερικῇ Ὀρθοδόξων Καρ-παθορρωσικῶν Κοινοτήτων.

Ὅθεν εἰς πίστωσιν καὶ βεβαίωσιν δίδοται τῷ εἰρημένῳ θεοφιλεστάτῳ Ἐπισκόπῳ Ἁγαθονικείας κυρίῳ Ὀρέστῃ Τσορνόκ τὸ παρὸν ἡμῶν Χειροτονητήριον Γράμμα.

Ὑπεγράφη αὐθημερὸν ἐν τοῖς Πατριαρχείοις Κωνσταντινουπόλεως.

120

Patriarchal Synod's Document of Consecration of The Most Reverend Bishop Orestes.

BY permission and exhortation of His All-Holiness the Oecumenical Patriarch Benjamin I, we the undersigned Metropolitans, of Sardes and Pisidia Germanos, of Eirenopolis Constantine, and of Laodicaea Dorotheos, who are members of the Holy and Sacred Patriarchal Synod of the Oecumenical Throne, having celebrated the eighteenth day of the month of September of the year of our Lord One Thousand Nine Hundred and Thirty Eight, in the Holy Patriarchal Church of the Glorious Great-Martyr Saint George the Trophy-Bearer, we have consecrated as Bishop, by the grace of the Holy Spirit, the Reverend among Presbyters ORESTES CHORNOCK, one of the clergymen of the Orthodox Carpatho-Russian Communities in America, who has been elevated to the office of Bishop by canonical votes of the Holy and Sacred Patriarchal Synod, with the honorary title of Bishop of the once illustrious Holy Diocese of Agathonikeia.

In the testimony and confirmation thereof, this our Letter of Consecration is given to the said Most Reverend Bishop of Agathonikeia Mgr. Orestes Chornock.

Subscribed on the same day in the Patriarchate of Constantinople.

+ GERMANOS, Metropolitan
    of Sardes and Pisidia,

+ CONSTANTINE, Metropolitan
    of Eirenopolis,

+ DOROTHEOS, Metropolitan
    of Laodicaea.

Dokument Patriaršoho Synoda o Chirotoniji Preosvjasčenňijšoho Episkopa Oresta.

S pozvolenijem i blahoslovenijem Jeho Svjat'išestva, Vselenskoho Patriarcha Venjamina I, my nižepodpisanny Mitropolity, Germanos, Sardes-skij i Pisidiaskij; Konstantin, Eirenopolis-skij i Dorothej, Laodicaea-skij, kotory jesme členami Svjatoho Patriaršeskoho Synoda Vselenskoho Prestola, posl'i soveršenija Božestvennoj Liturgii dnes, v Ned'il'u, osemnadcatoho dňa mįsjaca Septembra, hoda jeden tysjač devjat' sto tridcjat osmoho, Hospoda našeho, v Svjatoj Patriaršeskoj Cerkvi Sv. Slavnoho Veliko-Mučenika Georgija Pobidonosca, my vysvjatili za episkopa, blahodatiju Ducha Svjatoho, Vsesvitľijšoho svjasčennika Oresta Chornock, duchovnįka iz Karpatorusskich Pravoslavnych cerkovnych obščin v Ameriki, kotoryj byl vozvyšennyj na san Episkopa kanoničnymi holosami Svjat'ijšoho Patriaršeskoho Synoda, s počestnym titulom Episkopa koliś' slavnoj Diocezii — Agathonikeia.

V svid'inije i potverždenije seho, peredavajeme sej naš dokument vysvjasčenija — Jeho Preosvjasčenstvu, Episkopu Agathonikejskomu, Kir Orestu Chornock.

Podpisannyj v toj samyj deň v Patriaršestvi Konstantinohrada.

+ GERMANOS, Mitropolit
    Sardes-skij i Pisidia-skij,

+ KONSTANTIN, Mitropolit
    Eirenopolis-skij,

+ DOROTHEJ, Mitropolit
    Laodicaea-skij.

Upon returning to New York on October 19, 1938, the newly-consecrated bishop found a large crowd awaiting his arrival on the pier near 48th Street. Many priests and faithful wept openly that their almost ten years of struggle had not been in vain. They had at last "a bishop of their own heart" and theirs was the first Orthodox Carpatho-Russian Church to exist since 1646. The new bishop was presented with flowers by children from his Bridgeport parish, which was to be his diocesan seat, even though it was still involved in litigation. The Perth Amboy parish presented him with a chalice and the ancient words *Eis polla eti, Despota* echoed across the water.

On November 24, 1938, Thanksgiving Day, Bishop Orestes was installed formally by Patriarchal Exarch Archbishop Athenagoras. The program for the day began with Bishop Orestes first hierarchical celebration of the Divine Liturgy with installation sermons in Russian by Fr. Peter Molchany and in English by Fr. Joseph Mihaly. Following the installation ceremony, Fr. Stephen Varzaly, the Treasurer of the diocese read the "Patriarchal Letter of Appointment." The day ended with a testimonial dinner for the new bishop. The installation took place at "Saint John's Cathedral" as the church on Arctic Street was now being called, since Bishop Orestes had chosen it as his administrative seat and still performed most of the pastoral duties there.

The program book contained a history of the creation of the diocese, a brief biography of the bishop and an article calling upon the priests and faithful of the diocese to fulfill their spiritual obligations and to support their new bishop and their diocese, so that the installation would mark the beginning of a "golden age" for the Carpatho-Russian people and their church. At the age of fifty-five, when many today dream of retirement, Orestes Chornock was only beginning the greatest work of his earthly life.

An Interpretation of the "Celibacy Struggle" and the Events of 1938

In recent years several individuals have attempted an analysis of the "Bor'ba"—the struggle over the issues of "Latinization" and celibacy that rocked the Greek Catholic Church in America in the 1930s and whose evidence is still to be seen today. Some of the theories behind this struggle, which led to the consecration of Bishop Orestes and the establishment of an American Carpatho-Russian Orthodox Church, such as the affairs of the GCU and the "attempted takeover" of the Pittsburgh Eparchy by priests dissatisfied with Bishop Takach and his consultors (see note 91), as well as the issue of church charters, have already been examined. Each of the these theories, all proposed by persons generally inimical to Bishop Orestes and his diocese, have a weakness.

The consecration of Bishop Orestes and the establishment of his diocese in the Orthodox Church was not the result of any personal ambition on his part, nor on the part of the other leaders of the movement. Rather it was the result of a crisis of identity that has always existed in the Carpatho-Russian Greek Catholic Church. Although the "Borba" was precepitated by the celibacy provision of *Cum Data Fuerit* it had been brewing since the first Greek Catholic Carpatho-Russians arrived in America and had to deal with the Roman Catholic Church. The celibacy issue was only an external symptom of this far deeper question of identity: What exactly did it mean to be a member of the Greek Catholic Church? Fr. Molchany, speaking at the November 1937 Congress called himself a member of the "Russian Greek Catholic Eastern Rite Church" and as he pointed out Bishop Takach had begun to refer to himself as "a Roman Catholic of the Greek Rite."

The turmoil of the 1930s was centered on the spiritual identify of the Greek Catholic Church. Both sides insisted that they were the "true Greek Catholic Church" yet their viewpoints differed considerably. Was a Greek Catholic someone who belonged to the Roman Catholic Church and merely used the "Greek" Rite to worship as opposed to the Latin? Or was a Greek Catholic somone who belonged to a church that was separate from the Roman Church and only bound to it by the contract of "Union?" This issue was at the base of the rivalry betwen the Presov and Uzhorod seminaries, although it never reached a head in the Roman Catholic atmosphere of the old Austro-Hungarian Empire. In America with its freedom of the press and freedom of religion, the story was different.

Fr. Orestes and almost all of the priests of the new Carpatho-Russian Orthodox Greek Catholic Diocese were all of the Presov seminary; they identified with the new conditions of their flocks in America and their newfound love of democracy. The early issues of the *Vistnik* carried quotes from Patrick Henry, Benjamin Franklin and other Americans on "life, liberty and the pursuit of happiness" which they felt were being unfairly denied them by Bishop Takach, whom they saw as a carry-over from the servitude of the "Old Country" to the Hungarian landlords.

Bishop Takach and many of his key advisors (certainly not all the priests of the Pittsburg Eparchy who chose to remain in the Catholic Church) were for the most part graduates of the Uzhorod seminary, which in Europe identified with the dominant "Magyar" culture and the Roman Catholicism of that culture. In America, this group identified itself with the American Roman Catholic Church, whose power and influence impressed them and gave them a role model. Bishop Takach insisted that the central issue in the dispute was not celibacy but obedience to the "Holy Father" which took precedence over the "privileges of the Greek Catholic Church." This identification would culminate in the "Uniate Greek Catholic Church" with the removal of icon screens from the Church, the change of the calendar from the Julian to Gregorian, the introduction of Latin-Rite statues and devotions such as the "Way of the Cross" and even the removal of the

124

traditional triple-barred Cross in the 1950s.

For Bishop Orestes Chornock and the members of his diocese being "Greek Catholic" meant that one was a member of the "Greek Catholic Church" which existed apart from the Roman Catholic Church but was tied to it by the "contract" of Uzhorod.

At this point we must restate the identification of the "average" Carpatho-Russian with the Greek Catholic Church and its traditions. The Carpatho-Russian people did not possess a sense of national identity since they never had their own country, but were a subject people. The confusion over their name illustrates this. In America Carpatho-Russians referred to themselves as "Carpatho-Russians", "Uhro-Russians," "Uhro-Rusyns" ("Uhro" meaning "Hungarian", that is "from Hungary"), "Carpatho-Rusyns, "Rusyns," "Russians," and the Vatican insisted on calling them "Ruthenians"—a term which many found onerous. Nor did Carpatho-Russians have a national language. Most authors attempted to write in "Great Russian" with a strong admixture of Carpatho-Russian and even Church Slavonic words. The lack of a unified national language meant that there was also a lack of a standard alphabet. In America most newspapers used both Cyrillic and Latin scripts freely, with the Latin predominating.

The Hungarian government discouraged any display of Carpatho-Russian national feeling in the external forum. It was only in the Greek Catholic Church that the Carpatho-Russian was free to express his identity, and the Greek Catholic Church at the same time was his identity. Any change in the church was seen as a change of one's personal identity. Almost all Eastern Christians, subjected to hostile alien cultures, took refuge in their church. The Greek and Armenian Churches both became the guardians of national culture when the Turks threatened to destroy it.

As it is apparent from the letters it issued concerning the celibacy struggle, the Vatican simply could not understand this. In reading the documents sent to Bishop Takach through the apostolic delegate, one is struck with a sense of total bewilderment as to why a celibacy provision that initially affected only three individuals (three married seminarians) should bitterly divide the Pittsburgh Greek Catholic Eparchy. Used to dealing with Latin Rite Western oriented Catholics who usually accept change authorized by the proper authority, it was at a total loss in dealing with these "Greek Catholics."

For Bishop Orestes and his faithful, Rome had violated the Union of Uzhorod and attempted to radically alter their identity through the Latinization of the Greek Catholic Church. They came to realize that only by returning to the Orthodox Faith of their distant ancestors that their "Carpatho-Russian Greek Catholic" (the two terms were almost interchangeable just as "Greek" and "Orthodox" were in Ottoman Turkey) identity could be safeguarded. This also explains their reluctance to join the "Russian" Metropolia where Carpatho-Russians were turned into "Moskaly" (Muscovites).

For Bishop Takach and his supporters (though again it should be pointed out that many of the priests of the Pittsburgh Eparchy who remained with it disagreed, though silently), with their desire to be identified as "good Catholics" and win the approval of the American Catholic Church, being Greek Catholic became merely being a Roman Catholic "of the Greek (later 'Byzantine') Rite." Following the events of 1938, the "Uniate" Church became radically Latinized as its priests and faithful were reminded of "their Catholic obligation" first and the "Byzantine Rite" second.

The establishment of the Carpatho-Russian Orthodox diocese and the consecration of Bishop Orestes, as well as the eager Latinization of the Pittsburgh Eparchy by Bishop Takach and his successors, were the result of these two conflicting answers to the question of what it was to be a "Greek Catholic." The celibacy struggle would perhaps be better named the "struggle for Carpatho-Russian identity."

14. As Administrator of our
Diocese in 1936.

15. Fr. Peter E. Molchany, 1936.

16. "National Religious Congress" (Sobor) of November 1937 which elected Fr. Orestes Chornock to be the Bishop-elect of an Orthodox Carpatho-Russian Diocese.

Chapter 5

"RECEIVE THE PASTORAL STAFF"

The day before his solemn installation as bishop of the newly-canonized Orthodox Carpatho-Russian diocese, Bishop Orestes Chornock called for a priests' conference at the Barnum Hotel in Bridgeport. The new bishop had a great deal of work to do. The old ties with Rome had been cut forever. He had a church to build anew and the spirit of Orthodoxy to instill into his people. He had to remove the bitterness of ten years of struggle that was in the hearts of many and to heal their wounded spirits. He had to instill order and discipline where years of disorder and protest had weakened all respect for authority. It would not be an easy task. But it would be an impossible task without the support and cooperation of his priests.

Twenty-nine priests, many of them former "Uniates,"

assembled with their bishop to begin what they called "the new life in the diocese."[1] Fr. Peter Molchany and Fr. Stephen Varzaly called upon all of the priests who were currently holding offices in the diocese to resign from those offices. There would be new elections and appointments at this priests' conference, now that the diocese was Orthodox and had a canonical bishop. The following resignations were tendered: Fr. Stephen Varzaly—from Vicar-Chancellor, Fr. Peter Molchany—from Dean of the Pittsburgh Deanery, Fr. Joseph Mihaly—from Dean of the Youngstown Deanery, Fr. Irenaeus Dolhy—from Dean of the New York Deanery, and Fr. Basil Kurutz—from Dean of the Johnstown Deanery.

The resignations were accepted. The patriarchal documents were presented to the priests and inserted into the minutes of the conference. The following appointments were made by Bishop Orestes: Fr. Stephen Varzaly, treasurer; Fr. Joseph Mihaly, secretary; Fr. Irenaeus Dolhy, controller. Following the appointment of these officials of the new diocese by Bishop Orestes the election for vicar-general was held. Fr. Peter Molchany was nominated and unanimously approved by the priests. Additional members to the diocesan consistory were elected by the priests and a diocesan tribunal was set up. The diocese was restructured into six deaneries: New York, Scranton, Johnstown, Pittsburgh, Youngstown, and Chicago. The bishop was to appoint the deans and also a diocesan censor at a later time.

The next item to be discussed was a seminary. Even in the Uniate Church there was no seminary for training priests for the Greek Catholic Church in America. Arrangements were worked out either to send young men to a Roman Catholic seminary or even to Europe, to the seminaries of Presov or Uzhorod. Bishop Orestes felt that if the diocese was to grow it would need a seminary, where priests to serve it, educated in its purpose and mission, would be trained. The possibility of training priests in

Philadelphia was mentioned but nothing was resolved.

The diocesan newspaper, the *Vistnik-Messenger* was brought up. Each priest was to contribute $5.00 for the support of the paper. All agreed. Fr. Varzaly mentioned the lack of candidates for the priesthood in the diocese at the time. The reasons for this were debated but nothing was finally resolved. Several other matters were discussed among them the situation of the Carpatho-Russians still in Europe and the developments in Czechoslovakia. The conference ended with the singing of "Dostojno jest."

There would be many priests' conferences in the early years of the diocese. At almost each conference, Bishop Orestes would have to restate the need for order, the need for the priests to be above all spiritual men, the need for parishes to be truly churches of God. One incident at the priests' conference of June 4, 1940 in Pittsburgh reveals the problems that Bishop Orestes had to face in establishing canonical order in the diocese.

A church that had sought entrance into the diocese did not charter itself as a church, but rather as the "Brotherhood of Saint Nicholas" which was organized not for "worship" but for "recreation." The members of the parish felt that this would make it impossible for the "Uniates" to gain control of the church and "take it to Rome," since it legally was not a church at all but a social club. Furthermore, the priest of the parish had signed a ten-year "contract" with the parish council. When these facts were brought to light at the priests' conference, Bishop Orestes, who had spoken privately about correcting these conditions in the parish with no result, gave notice to the pastor that unless the charter was dissolved and the church re-incorporated as a church for the worship of God, and his "contract" was cancelled, the parish could not be in the diocese.[2] Each parish had to sign the diocesan by-laws as well as each priest as a sign of support for the diocese and the bishop. Those responsible for incidents like the above, and there were many instances when the authority of Bishop Orestes

129

was challenged, caused a great deal of harm to the unity of the new diocese. Bishop Orestes though, did not take personal offense, but was always willing to forgive those who repented. He believed in looking to the future rather than looking backwards at the hurts of the past.

The "Carpatho-Russian Youth" Organization

The first diocesan Sobor (as the Congress of November 1937 has come to be recognized), called for the establishment of a diocesan youth organization to be named the "Sons and Daughters of the Eastern Church" that would have branches in each parish and an annual national convention. It purpose was to provide "active and aggresive leadership in our parishes" and a magazine to be called "Carpatho-Russian Youth."

In April of 1939, the first issue of the magazine "Carpatho-Russian Youth" appeared in a well printed format, featuring articles on historical and contemporary subjects, as well as news of each chapter. Especially featured was the consecration and installation of Bishop Orestes that took place the previous November.

In October of 1939, the youth organization held its first national convention in Johnstown, Pennsylvania. The original name of the organization gave way to "Carpatho-Russian Youth" the title of its magazine, and the group was popularly called the "C.R.Y."[3] At the convention Bishop Orestes made the opening address, since he believed in the organization and also knew it would be the young people of the diocese whose faith and whose enthusiasm would heal the wounds of the "Bor'ba." He would always try to be present at the organization's convention.

The convention adopted a set of by-laws including a symbol: a double-headed eagle clutching a three-barred cross and a torch, a star enclosed in a circle were centered on the eagle design. Choir competition ended the event on Sunday evening October 8.

A second C.R.Y. convention was held in 1940, in Perth Amboy on August 9-10. At this convention Bishop Orestes demonstrated his faith in the young people of his diocese. The "Carpatho-Russian Youth" magazine, which had shown such promise the previous year was not being published. The C.R.Y. owed the printer $669.14 and the National Treasury of the group only contained $37.48! The delegates themselves collected $265.00. When Bishop Orestes became aware of the problem he personally donated, out of his own funds $300.00 to help cover the remainder of the debt.

During World War II, the activities of the C.R.Y. on the national level stopped totally. In many parishes though local chapters still continued to function as best as they could.

The Establishment of a Seminary

One of the problems facing the new diocese from its outset was a shortage of trained qualified priests and the lack of a seminary. This was one of the first priorities of Bishop Orestes. He felt that for the diocese to grow it would need priests who were drawn from its own churches and who embraced its goals and ideals.

At the time of the consecration of Bishop Orestes several young men were being privately tutored for ordination. This was at best a response to a crisis situation and was recognized as unsatisfactory. In 1940, temporary quarters for the seminary were obtained at Saint Nicholas Church on 10th Street in New York. Internal difficulties over the exact relationship of the seminary to the parish caused the seminary to be moved to a farm in Nicholson, Pennsylvania that was acquired for this purpose. Living conditions here were not suitable and in 1941 Bishop Orestes opened his home in Bridgeport to ten diocesan seminarians. Bishop Orestes personally oversaw the operation of the seminary during its years there, teaching the students, overseeing discipline and even sharing the expense of its operation.[4] Many of the priests trained in Bridgeport under the eye of Bishop Orestes are recognized as exemplars of the priesthood in their years of service to the diocese.

The Vistnik-Messenger

Another problem facing Bishop Orestes and the diocese was the diocesan newspaper the *Vistnik-Messenger*. The newspaper was discussed at almost every clergy conference and at the diocesan sobor of 1940. Its biggest problem was a lack of funds. Fr. Varzaly assumed full control of the newspaper in 1940, both editing and publishing it. The *Vistnik* of the early 1940s no longer carried the fiery denunciations of Rome as it had in the "independent" days of the diocese. There was news of world events, an emphasis on the "Russian" heritage of the Carpatho-Russian people, this through the influence of Fr. Varzaly who became impressed with the victories of the Soviet army during the war. There were both English and Carpatho-Russian articles carrying news of events in the diocese as well as sermons and polemical articles against the "Uniate" Church.

The Second Diocesan Sobor

On August 7 and 8, 1940, the second diocesan "Sobor" was held in Perth Amboy, New Jersey. In addition to discussing the seminary, the newspaper and the lack of funds facing the diocese, the delegates voted unanimously to add the word "Orthodox" to the official name of the diocese and re-affirmed their commitment to the Orthodox Faith.[5]

The Bridgeport Cathedral Church Is Lost In Court

The Arctic Street property of Saint John the Baptist Cathedral in Bridgeport, as the parish was now called because Bishop Orestes had his seat there, had been involved with court litigation since February 1932. The case was finally concluded in February 1944 before the Connecticut State Supreme Court. The final verdict was a bitter blow for Bishop Orestes and the faithful of the Church. The court ruled that the property, which had for three decades been the bishop's home, be awarded to the Uniates since the charter of the church stated it was "united with Rome."[6] Almost immediately the faithful of the Bridgeport parish followed Bishop Orestes, with the exception of a few families, and worked to finance totally on their own, through the sale of bonds primarily, a new and impressive "Cathedral Church" still called Saint John the Baptist on Mill Hill Avenue. This was accomplished by 1946. The large rectory next to the church served as the episcopal residence as well as the seminary.

The years of World War II curtailed the activities of Bishop Orestes as well as the administration of the diocese. No Sobor could be called because of the difficulty of travel. And the bishop himself had a great deal of difficulty in traveling. Life continued on in the diocese with everyone doing their part for the war effort as well as praying for its end.

The "Uniate" Reaction to the Canonization of the Diocese

The year 1938, with its consecration of Bishop Orestes, ended the "celibacy struggle" in the Uniate Pittsburgh Eparchy. On October 12 of that year, Bishop Takach in a pastoral letter spoke of the need for reorganizing the spiritual life of the Pittsburgh Eparchy "now that the fight is over."[7] The G.C.U. made one last attempt to have the papal authorities recall the celibacy provision of "Cum Data Fuerit." George Ferrio, Dr. Peter Zeedick, and John Sekarak, the President of the G.C.U., left on September 6, 1938 to meet with persons influential in the affairs of the European Uniate Church, finally meeting with the pope himself. Nothing of any value was accomplished by the trio.[8] Earlier on July 26, 1938, Fr. Peter Molchany was ousted as spiritual advisor of the G.C.U. and Fr. Varzaly had been replaced by Michael Roman as editor in 1937. Under the editorial leadership of Michael Roman, the former supporter of Bishop Orestes in the "independent" days of the diocese, the organization drew nearer to the position of Bishop Takach.[9] At the 1940 G.C.U. convention Bishop Takach was invited to address the delegates and only Uniates were admitted to the convention. About the only evidence that there was still some anti-celibacy feeling in the Uniate Eparchy of Pittsburgh was the election of John Yurcisin, a staunch traditionalist and foe of celibacy, to be the editor of the *Sokol* section of *ARV*. He soon left the position to study for the priesthood under Bishop Orestes.

The early 1940s was a time of organization for the diocese which had many ideas about spreading the Orthodox Faith among Carpatho-Russians, but which was frustrated by a lack of funds and the difficulties imposed by the war. Yet in establishing the C.R.Y. organization and the seminary and emphasizing the need for cooperation and hard work, Bishop Orestes planted seeds that would come to fruit later in his life.

In leaving the Uniate Church, Bishop Orestes personally left behind all of the pain of the "Bor'ba." As one of his parishioners said, he never uttered a bad word about Bishop Takach or any of the other members of the Pittsburgh diocese. Instead he believed in looking to the future, seeing what was on the horizon for his diocese and its priests and people whom he loved.

17. First class of the Diocesan Seminary in New York City in
1940, shown with Bishop Orestes.

18. Masthead of *Vistnik*.

Chapter 6

"A HOUSE DIVIDED"

Bishop Orestes had always had an overwhelming sense of loyalty to his diocese and its priests and people. This sense of loyalty was at the same time his greatest strength and his greatest weakness. In the later years of the 1940s, it was to cause him a great deal of personal hurt and threaten the existence of the diocese. Yet in the end his personal integrity and his faith overcame all of the crises and the diocese would begin an era of great progress by 1950.

The "Varzaly Schism"

Fr. Stephen Varzaly, as we have seen, was one of the prime movers in leading the struggle against Bishop Takach in his role as editor of the *ARV* and through the *Vistnik* was instrumental in the return of the diocese to the Orthodox Church. Fr. Varzaly had taken over full editorial responsibility for the diocesan newspaper *Vistnik* as well as serving as "publisher" in 1940. In reading the *Vistnik* during the war years, one becomes aware of growing emphasis placed on the "Russian peoples' " struggle against Hitler and with things "Soviet" in general. For instance, the July 10, 1941 issue of the *Vistnik* carried on the front page the "Speech of Stalin to the Russian People" with "Moscow" given in the dateline. The paper no longer spoke of "Rus" as Carpatho-Russians referred to their homeland, but of "Rossija." Carpatho-Russians had always maintained that they were not "Great Russians" or "Moskaly" (Muscovites) even though from time to time they became enamored of "Great Russian" culture and language. The paper also carried news of parish events, articles on various aspects of the Orthodox Faith and polemical materials directed against the "Uniate" Greek Catholic Church (whose press responded in kind against the Orthodox).

Fr. Varzaly came to feel that since the Carpatho-Russians were akin to the "Great Russians" the diocese should be under the jurisdiction of the Moscow Patriarchate.

The opportunity for this to happen occurred in the closing days of the war, when representatives of the Moscow Patriarchate visited Bishop Orestes. The Patriarchal Exarchate in America was not very large, not in comparison with the American "Metropolia" which had come into existence after the Russian Revolution. The Patriarchal representatives offered to make Bishop Orestes a metropolitan if he would bring his diocese under the jurisdiction of Moscow to be a "base of operations" against the Metropolia.[1]

Bishop Orestes flatly refused, stating his desire to remain loyal to the Ecumenical Patriarch of Constantinople, who had consecrated him and canonized the diocese. In addition, he felt with others that the Carpatho-Russians had never been under the jurisdiction of Moscow when they were Orthodox but under Kiev which was then subject to Constantinople.[2]

Fr. Varzaly was furious that the offer was rejected and began attacking publicly in the *Vistnik,* Bishop Orestes, the Ecumenical Patriarch, and anyone who disagreed with him. After repeated warnings Bishop Orestes censured Fr. Varzaly and dismissed him from the diocese.

This was not the end of the matter however. The diocesan newspaper, the *Vistnik,* continued to appear issued by Fr. Varzaly, who refused to give up his position as editor. Bishop Orestes had trusted Fr. Varzaly implictly in setting up the newspaper legally. Now Bishop Orestes found out that Fr. Varzaly was the legal owner of the *Vistnik* and not the diocese. There was nothing he could do to stop the flow of articles attacking him, the priests and people who were loyal to him.

In addition, Fr. Varzaly was a popular figure from the days of the "Bor'ba" and there were, unfortunately, too many "anarchists" among the clergy and people left over from the "Bor'ba" who found the bishop's insistence on canonical order and procedure personally affronting. They were only too ready to join in the attack on the Bishop and the diocese. The diocese was in serious trouble.

The Establishment of the "Church Messenger"

In September 1946, Bishop Orestes called for a conference of diocesan clergy in Johnstown, Pensylvania, to take steps to fight against the threat posed to the diocese by Fr. Varzaly and his followers.[3] At this conference each priest was asked to take an oath of fidelity to the bishop, and the actions of Fr. Varzaly were condemned by the priests present.

We have seen the role of the newspapers in the Carpatho-Russian communities already and Fr. Vazzaly had a powerful weapon in his *Vistnik*. To counter this threat each of the priests at the conference contributed $25.00 to begin a new diocesan newspaper that was called the

Cerkovnyj Vistnik, that is *The Church Messenger.* The first issue of the *Church Messenger* published on September 10, 1946 contained a scathing denunciation of Fr. Varzaly written by Fr. Constantine Auroroff. The article entitled "Who is Fr. Varzaly?" went back to his 1928 trip to Florida, taken to recover his voice, on funds donated by Bishop Takach and the priests of the Pittsburgh Eparchy. He accused him of duplicity during the "Bor'ba," recalling that he had been reconciled with Bishop Takach only to be suspended again when the parishoners of his Rankin church made him recant. He denounced the "Varzaly Vistnik," as the old Vistnik was being called, in these words: "The Varzaly Vistnik' reminds us of a Moscovite, bolshevik magazine, where the name of 'Comrade Stalin' (and only his!) stands on every page . . ."[4]

An English article, explaining the "raison d' être" of the *Church Messenger* warned the faithful that the old *Vistnik* was completely owned by Fr. Varzaly and that any funds sent to it were his.[5] The article made three accusations against the former priest of the diocese. It accused him of attempting to impose his will on the Bishop with the ultimate purpose of being the "Big Boss." Also using sensational and falsified stories in the *Vistnik,* he increased the sales of the paper, making more money for himself. Finally, it gave Fr. Varzaly's third objective as failing to become the "leader" of the diocese; he tried to divide it into factions so that the diocese would cease to exist.[6]

The front page of the first issue of the *Church Messenger* contained a moving letter from Bishop Orestes. The Bishop, addressing the editorial committee of the *Church Messenger,* spoke of the attacks of Fr. Varzaly in his "private newspaper" against the priests and faithful of the diocese. The Bishop said, "I did not seek the episcopal mitre, and none other than Fr. Varzaly himself begged me to become bishop . . ." He spoke of the "crown of thorns" that Fr. Varzaly had placed now upon his head. Of how in his pride he had told Bishop Orestes, "I gave you the mitre, I can take it from you!" He spoke of how he would not, through the diocese, serve the "dictator Stalin" or the "almighty pope." Bishop Orestes then went on to say that he had been chosen by the "people" and that the people gave him birth as a bishop, "I am their child." When one laughed at the child, as Fr. Varzaly was doing to him, one insulted the parents who gave birth: in the case of the bishop, the people of the diocese. The bishop further stated: "I do not serve Fr. Varzaly but the people of the diocese!"[7]

The text of this letter shows that Bishop Orestes felt betrayed by Fr. Varzaly and that he was truly wearing "a crown of thorns" as a result of the priest's actions.

The Third Diocesan Sobor

The war years made it impossible for the Sobor to convene. However, Bishop Orestes issued the call for the Sobor to take place on December 11, 1946 in Bridgeport. As to be expected, the matter of Fr. Varzaly was the main item discussed and as a result of the "propaganda" of the *Vistnik,* there were several who demanded to know why a council had not been called earlier, and also questioned the bishop's handling of financial matters.[8]

Fr. Peter Molchany, the vicar general of the diocese, spoke in defense of the bishop. He explained that the war and the loss of the Bridgeport parish made it impossible to call a council any earlier than this, and that it was he, at a priests' conference in 1945, who suggested that the Sobor take place in the beautiful new Bridgeport church. He reminded the delegates of how important it was to show respect to the bishop of the diocese, whose spiritual leadership and spiritual commands should be gladly obeyed. The vicar-general did not shrink back from addressing the actions of Fr. Varzaly, prompted he said by his conscience, regardless of whether or not what he said was pleasing to the delegates. The "war of the Rev. Varzaly," as he called it, was begun by Fr. Varzaly, "who always desires struggle and war" and to "plunge our people into the flames of hatred and self-determination." He refuted the attacks of Fr. Varzaly on the Ecumenical Patriarchate and asked how the Fathers of the Church and such popular Carpatho-Russian saints as Saint Nicholas could be termed "Greek mud" as they, like the patriarch, were also Greek; Fr. Varzaly had applied this term to the churches of the Patriarchate.

Bishop Orestes, in responding to the attacks of Fr. Varzaly, presented a financial report to the delegates of the Sobor. The report revealed that the diocese over the past three years had expenses totalling $19,674.93. The corresponding income was $12.752.25. This left a deficit of $6.922.68, which Bishop Orestes paid out of his own funds. The delegates were scandalized upon hearing this report in view of the accusations of Fr. Varzaly against the bishop. The Sobor unanimously placed itself on record as rejecting any insinuation that the bishop misappropriated any funds. Several priests and lay delegates spoke out against the actions of Fr. Varzaly and in behalf of the bishop. The bishop summed up the session in these words: "I accepted the office of bishop to lead the people in establishing an Orthodox diocese, not to be regarded as a 'champion of the people.'"

Some of the delegates wanted Fr. Varzaly to be present in the hope that he would submit to the bishop and make peace. However, the bishop reminded them that they did not have the authority to override his censure of Fr. Varzaly and that Fr. Varzaly, to be re-instated, would have to submit to canonical process. A group of lay delegates was authorized by the bishop to inform Fr. Varzaly of this, if they wished, but his presence was forbidden at the council, since he was no longer a priest of the diocese until he sought forgiveness.

Early in the 1940, Bishop Orestes transferred Fr. Joseph Mihaly to the Bridgeport parish from Saint Michael's Church in Binghamton, New York. The Binghamton parish had just won a favorable court ruling against

Bishop Takach and his Pittsburgh Eparchy and Fr. Mihaly had been instrumental in the favorable outcome. Bishop Orestes transferred Fr. Mihaly back to Bridgeport with the hope that his Binghamton experience would help in the upcoming appeals for the Arctic Street property of the Bridgeport parish. Fr. Mihaly began to study law at Yale University in preparation for the case, eventually being admitted to the bar. Bishop Orestes, though involved with the affairs of the diocese, officially continued to be the pastor of the Bridgeport parish, assisted by Fr. Mihaly, and the Bridgeport parish was, through the presence of the bishop, the cathedral church of the diocese.

Though the final court ruling regarding the Arctic Street property of the Bridgeport parish did not come until 1944, it was becoming apparent that Saint John the Baptist on Arctic Street was going to be awarded to the Uniates. A new property on Mill Hill Avenue in Bridgeport was aquired and fund raising was begun for a new church while the case was still pending. If funds were raised under the name of Saint John's on Arctic Street there was a possibility that they could be, as assets of the church, awarded to the Uniates together with the property, since the case was still pending. The parishoners began to raise funds under the legal name of the "American Sons and Daughters of Carpatho-Russia" to safeguard their interests from any adverse court ruling. When the Arctic Street church was lost, the Mill Hill Avenue Church legally continued to owe its existence to the "American Sons and Daughters of Carpatho-Russia" as the parishoners never rechartered themselves as "Saint John the Baptist Church."[9]

Early in 1947, a disagreement arose between Fr. Mihaly and the parish council of the Bridgeport church over the question of a substitute priest in the absences of Fr. Mihaly.[10] The parish council requested that Fr. Mihaly be transferred and another priest assigned to the parish by the bishop. Bishop Orestes informed the council that since it was already Lent, he could not make any changes and, in addition, had no immediate replacement. However, he did promise to replace Fr. Mihaly within three months.[11] Bishop Orestes felt that the request to transfer Fr. Michaly was based on only personal reasons on the part of some members on the council. He, therefore, refused to give a written statement to the council that he would replace him. The parish council, with majority approval of the entire congregation, demanded that Fr. Mihaly be removed in one month's time or else he would be "put out." Moreover Bishop Orestes would be "put out" as well.[12]

Bishop Orestes was caught between his love for the Bridgeport parish as its pastor for over three decades and his responsibility to his priest as a bishop. Perhaps the Bridgeport parishioners felt that he would choose them, since he was their priest. But his overwhelming sense of loyalty as a bishop dictated that he stand with Fr. Mihaly. The reponse of the parish council was to lock him out of the church.

Bishop Orestes, Fr. Mihaly and those parishoners who remained royal to him found that because of the church charter they had no choice but to leave the Mill Hill Avenue church, the church that the bishop had led the struggle for after the loss of Arctic Street. Those who remained loyal to him went with him and in a short time founded, or perhaps we should say, "refounded" Saint John the Baptist Church on Broadbridge Avenue. The diocesan bishop no longer had a cathedral church. The Mill Hill Avenue parish began searching for a new pastor from among the priests of the diocese, but all remained loyal to their bishop. Eventually the parish came to be a member of the Russian Orthodox "Metropolia."

The Founding of the A.C.R.Y

Despite the tragedy of Bridgeport for the diocese and for Bishop Orestes personally, the year 1947 did see some positive beginnings that would eventually bring about the end of the activities of Fr. Varzaly and his supporters who sought to captialize on the loss of the Bridgeport Cathedral on Mill Hill Avenue. The first of these signs of growth was the organization of the American Carpatho-Russian Youth, known popularly as the A.C.R.Y.

The A.C.R.Y. was born from the remains of the earlier C.R.Y. organization. At the Third Diocesan Sobor in December of 1946, the delegates called for the re-establishment of the diocesan youth organization that had been dormant during the war years. On May 4, 1947, 250 delegates from twenty C.R.Y. chapters met with the authorization of Bishop Orestes in Johnstown to reorganize the group. August 29-31 of the same year was chosen as the date for the convention and Pittsburgh as its site.[14]

The convention came to be known as the third A.C.R.Y. convention (the 1939 and 1940 C.R.Y. conventions were numbered as the first two). This convention dealt a bitter blow to Fr. Varzaly and his hopes of bringing the diocese under the jurisdiction of Moscow. Since his censure and canonical dismissal by the Bishop, Fr. Varzaly's paper the *Vistnik* had become openly pro-Soviet, taking stories from *Izvestia*, glorifying Stalin and praising the Soviet Union as the country of hope and promise to which all the nations were looking. In response to this the A.C.R.Y. convention in Pittsburgh officially changed the name of the organization from "Carpatho-Russian Youth" to "American Carpatho-Russian Youth." The constitution and by-laws of the organization called for it to foster not only the Orthodox faith but also "true Americanism, loyalty and allegiance to the government of the United States of America."[15] The organization also passed a resolution with six points aimed at the editor of the "Rankin *Vistnik*." Among them a declaration of loyalty to the United States' government and the condemnation of all "isms" except for "Americanism." A second point condemned all attempts "made to affiliate our diocese with Moscow." The point continued, "If any change of affiliation is to be made by our

143

diocese it should be to a canonically established American Orthodox Patriarch, and then only on condition that the autonomous rights and privileges that our diocese enjoys at the present time be preserved."

The third point condemned those "individuals who have placed their own personal interests above those of the diocese and have thereby caused and are fostering disunity and a ruinous faith-destroying conflict to the detriment of our Church, diocese and people." This was a reference especially to the work of Fr. Varzaly. The resolution called for the upcoming Sobor to be held in Johnstown to bring finally peace back to the diocese. Its fifth point called for the establishment of a seminary and pledged financial support of the seminary. The sixth point called for the young people in the parishes to take a more active part in the diocese and in local parish affairs, working together with the older people in each parish.

After the convention the A.C.R.Y. organization began to grow with many new chapters. Its activities were given a prominent place in the *Church Messenger*. Fr. Varzaly's following was largely among the older "immigrant" generation. The children of this generation totally rejected his message as this convention reveals. He had no support among the younger members of the diocese, who centered themselves around Bishop Orestes.

Fr. Varzaly and "the People's Church"

At the 1947 Sobor of the Diocese, held on December 16 in Johnstown, the lay committee that went to see Fr. Varzaly after the previous year's Sobor informed the delegates that Fr. Varzaly would not change his thoughts, nor would he submit to Bishop Orestes. The delegation was told of the benefits of placing the diocese under Bishop Adam (Philipovsky, who in 1943 left the "Metropolia" for the Patriarchal Exarchate of Moscow).[16] The 1947 Sobor delegates also issued a resolution similar in tone to that issued by the A.C.R.Y. earlier in the year. The resolution condemned communism and declared the loyalty of the diocese to the "democratic form of government of our beloved country."[17]

By 1949 Fr. Varzaly came to realize that Bishop Orestes was not going to step down and that the Carpatho-Russian Orthodox Greek Catholic Diocese was not going to leave the Patriarchate of Constantinople for that of Moscow. In fact through the efforts of the priests loyal to Bishop Orestes and the steady progress of the A.C.R.Y. the movement of Fr. Varzaly was beginning to lose momentum. The *Church Messenger* attacked the movement at every turn, from reminding naturalized citizens of their oath of allegiance to the United States to reprinting an article from the *Pittsburgh Press* (printed in the Press on Sunday, January 25, 1948) which revealed the pro-Soviet activities of Fr. Varzaly.

Fr. Varzaly proceeded to call a "People's Church Congress" which was attended by representatives of fourteen parishes and priests who were discontented with Bishop Orestes. This "Congress" met on July 25 and 26 in 1949 and was soundly condemned by the *Church Messenger*, Bishop Orestes, and the diocesan board of trustees in the July 15 edition of the paper. The movement was condemned as sectarian and with its emphasis on the "People's Church" seen as totally rejecting the Orthodox canonical tradition which places the lawful bishop at the head of the church.

Fr. Varzaly had intended to place the "Carpatho-Russian People's Church" under the jurisdiction of the Moscow Patriarchate. However one month before the start of the "Congress," the House of Representatives Committee on Un-American Activities issued a report exposing Fr. Varzaly as a communist sympathizer and the *Vistnik* as a paper which followed the "Communist party line."[18] This was of course no secret to anyone who had been reading the *Vistnik* but the exposure by the House of Representatives frightened the members of the "People's

145

Church Congress" into settling for a union with the Russian Orthodox Greek Catholic "Metropolia" instead of directly with the Moscow Patriarchate.

The Metropolia accepted the Carpatho-Russian People's Church incorporating it into a "Carpatho-Russian Administration" in 1951 that would for years cause ill feelings between the Metropolia and the Carpatho-Russian Diocese of Bishop Orestes.

Bishop Orestes, acting on the advice of the Ecumenical Patriarch Exarch in the United States, Archbishop Michael, invited Fr. Varzaly and five other suspended priests of the diocese who were involved with the "People's Church" to attend a conference on August 9, 1950 at the archbishop's offices in New York if they desired to be reinstated into the diocese. None of the priests appeared. On August 10, Archbishop Michael issued the following encyclical:

Encyclical Letter

of

His Eminence, the Most Reverend Archbishop of New York

MICHAEL

Apostolic Delegate and Supreme Patriarchal Representative

of

The Ecumenical Patriarchate of Constantinople in America

To All of the Carpatho-Russian Orthodox Clergy and Laity in America

August 10, 1950

Grace and Peace from God Our Father and from the Lord, Jesus Christ!

Since my arrival in this great and beloved country, it was my earnest desire to contact all of you through a pastoral letter. Owing, however, to my duties to supervise over three hundred and twenty Greek Orthodox parishes, scattered throughout North and South America, I was unable, up to the present moment, to fulfill my desire. I now take great pleasure in finding the opportunity to write you this letter, through your Bishop, the Most Reverend Orestes, and to convey to you all the blessings and cordial wishes, for your welfare and spiritual progress, of our great Leader, His All-Holiness the Ecumenical Patriarch Athenagoras, and His Holy and Sacred Synod in Constantinople.

Dear Brethren and Children in Our Lord Jesus Christ!

The Ecumenical Patriarchate, this centre of the Orthodox Church and our Common Mother, is always greatly interested in you all. Its only joy and satisfaction is to hear that you walk steadily in the Orthodox Faith and live a life worthy of our Orthodox tradition. And we, our humility, as the chief representative of the Ecumenical Patriarchate in this country, are at every moment ready to assist you in all matters concerning your Carpatho-Russian Communties and your Parishes. Every one of you, whether he belongs to the Clergy or the laity, will always be welcomed to the Archdiocese for every question, personal or otherwise.

My only wish and sacred desire is to know that you are united under your Bishop, the Most Reverend Orestes, who, as it is well known, was elected and consecrated by the Holy and Sacred Synod of the Ecumenical Patriarchate. I know that some misunderstendings have taken place in the past amongst you. And I want, through this letter, which is being addressed to you through your Bishop and our beloved Brother in Christ, the Most Reverend Orestes, to ask you all to forget the past and start a new period of ecclesiastical life and work, by coming closer together and being united with the bonds of Christian love and mutual understanding. Do not forget that all of us represent in this country the One, Holy, Catholic and Apostolic Orthodox Church; that our sacred duty towards the Church is to be united and avoid every division, which is always to the detriment of the prestige and good name of our Orthodox Church.

Trust your Bishop. Go to him for the solution of your problems. Leave the judgments in his hands. Be always mindful of the fact that "where the Bishop is, there is the Church," according to St. Ignatius, Bishop of Antioch. Have confidence in his decisions. He is kind-hearted; he is a good Christian and a lenient Bishop, and I am sure that he will settle every difference of yours, having as a rule — Christian love.

Hoping that you will listen to my voice and act according to our common faith and the capital virtue of the Christian life, i. e. charity, I invoke upon you all every blessing from Almighty God.

Yours very sincerely in Christ,

✠ Archbishop MICHAEL

147

On November 24, 1950, Patriarch Athenagoras who had been instrumental in the founding of the diocese, issued the following encyclical confirming that of Archbishop Michael:

Patriarchal Encyclical

HIS HOLINESS

ATHENAGORAS I

BY THE GRACE OF GOD

ARCHBISHOP OF CONSTANTINOPLE AND ECUMENICAL PATRIARCH

✠

No. 634

TO THE REVEREND CLERGY AND THE LAITY OF THE CARPATHO-RUSSIAN ORTHODOX CHURCH IN AMERICA

May the Grace and Peace of God be with you!

Our Holy Mother, the Great Church of Christ, following dutifully the command of our Lord and Saviour, Who gave His peace to the Disciples, and through them to all Christians, has set as one of Her main objectives the cultivation and promotion of peace, and love, and harmony, among its pious Christians, for their benefit and salvation.

It has been brought formally to our attention, and to the attention of our Holy Synod, that certain misunderstandings have arisen among you, which have alienated the desired peace and brotherly love. Through this Patriarchal Letter, therefore, and by the decision of our Holy and Sacred Synod, we urge all of you wholeheartedly to return to the Fold and place yourselves under the jurisdiction of His Grace, the Most Reverend Bishop of Agathonikia ORESTES, and reinstate yourselves in full unity with His Grace and among yourselves. We urge you to forget the past and extend your hands to each other in sincere cooperation, for the benefit and greater progress of the Holy and so beloved to us Carpatho-Russian Orthodox Church, of your communities, and of all the clergy and laity.

Our affection and our sincere interest for you and in your efforts to organize and establish your Church, is well known to you. We feel confident, therefore, that our paternal suggestion will reach your hearts and will influence your policy, particularly on the occasion of the approaching Christmas Holydays.

With our best wishes for Advent and for the Christmas Holydays, we invoke upon you the Grace and Mercy of God.

✠ ATHENAGORAS

Ironically, the "Carpatho-Russian People's Church" following the prophecy of Gamaliel (Acts 5 38), lasted not even a decade as an "administration" before one by one its parishes began to return to Bishop Orestes as did several of its priests. The "Carpatho-Russian People's Church" today exists only as a bad memory for those who lived through the strife and bitterness that it caused.

Other Developments of the Late 1940s

The seeds planted by the bishop before the war began to take root, despite the "Varzaly Schism." The A.C.R.Y. was growing steadily and spreading the ideals of Bishop Orestes through its conventions, its *A.C.R.Y. Annual,* which appeared first in 1948 and its organization of new chapters which gave a sense of unity to the parishes of the diocese. The seminary was forced out of Bridgeport when the parish left the diocese in 1947. A temporary set-up was arranged for at the University of Pennsylvania with the students attending classes there and being affiliated with the Hawk Run Pennsylvania parish. Also other Orthodox seminaries were used to help train priests but none of these arrangements was to prove satisfactory. The 1948 A.C.R.Y. Convention called for a permanent seminary to be established as well as the establishment of a diocesan center, especially needed since the loss of the Bridgeport Mill Hill Avenue parish was a diocesan cathedral. (The arrangements in Bridgeport had only really been stop-gap anyway: since it was Bishop Orestes' parish as a priest, he elected to remain there as bishop. The war years prevented any move of the diocesan see even if Bishop Orestes had desired it, which at the time he did not).

The encyclical letters of Archbishop Michael and Patriarch Athenagoras, together with the love and faith of Bishop Orestes in the people of the diocese, especially the members of the A.C.R.Y., provided the means of turning the labors and suffering of the late 1940s into a joyous harvest in the following decade.

19. Fr. Stephen Varzaly.

CERKONYJ VISTNIK

ЦЕРКОВНЫЙ ВѢСТНИКЪ

THE CHURCH MESSENGER

| Volume One | McKEES ROCKS, PA., September 19, 1946 | Issue 1 |

Eparchiaľnaja Kanceľarija

Sept. 10, 1946

Slava Isusu Christu!

Redakcionnomu Komitetu "Cerkovnaho Vistnika".

L'ubeznyje moji Otcy Duchovnyje:

Na svjaščenničeskom Sobori vo Johnstown-i svjaščenstvo izbralo Vas za redaktorov našej eparchiaľnoj gazety—"Cerkovnyj Vistnik." Sim putem ja, jako Archipastyr' Vaš, podtverždaju sije Vaše izbranije i udiľaju Vam svoje Archijerejskoje blahoslovenije.

My pereživajeme teper' lukavyje časy. Po našej nedaľnozorkosti i dobroti my dozvolili "Vistniku", privatnoj gazeti o. Varzalija, vstupiti do zahradki našej Eparchiji i teper eta gazeta napadajet ne liš na moju skromnuju osobu, no i na mojich svjaščennikov s ich bohobojnymi virnikami.

Ja ne hľadal episkopskoj koruny, i nikto inšij jak sam o. Varzaly umoľal mene statisja episkopom, inače, jak tohda tverdil tot že o. Varzaly, naša molodaja Eparchija rozpadnetsja. Ne dumal ja, ľubeznyje moji otcy, devjať ľit tomu nazad, čto moja episkopska koruna dakoli obernetsja dľa mene vo ternovyj vinec. A ono tak stalosja: vo ternovyj vinec obľekli mene o. Varzaly, tot, kotoroho ja vsehda miloval, voschvaľal, tituly daval. Osmijujet teper' on mene, pľujet na mene i obišča jet svojim nennoho žialennym priveržencam rapisati obč mňi takija vešči, čto "až voloxja vstanut na holovi."

Ot počatku svojeho episkopstva ja ne imiř pokoja ot o. Varzaly-a. Vo svojej hordosti-pychi sej ozloblennyj duchovnik vsehda hojkal, kričal na mene: "ja dal tebi koronu, ja ju ot tebe i otberu." Ale Hospoď Boh nahorodil mene talantom terpinija. Ja znaju, jak terpiti ot svojeho mladenčestva, bo iz chudobnaho rodu pochožu ja. Ja i terpil vsi ličnyje ponosy ot o. Varzaly-a. Nikomu ne skaržilsja. Jako episkop ja imil pravo davniji o. Varzalija za našej Eparchiji vypustiti, no toho ja ne ďilal, daby ľudi zloj voli ne podumali, čto ja lično vymstilsja nad o. Varzaly-em.

Ja znaju terpiti svoji ličnyju potuplenija, no ja ne možu, ba i ne chočn sterpiti kohda kto potupľajet, na smich, na publiku vystavľajet moj milyj i nevinnyj karpato-russkij narod. Kohda naši bratja-uniaty čitajut teperišnyj Varzalevskij Vistnik, oni ne budut smichi robiti iz mene, ibo ja ne zaslan tut do Eparchiji ani diktatorom Stalinom, ani "rimohučšem" papoj Rimskim. Mene izbral NAROD. Narod mene porodil, jako episkopa. Ja jeho ďitina. Kohda nad ďitinoj smichi robiš, jak to ďilajet o. Varzaly, to oskorbľaješ, čest uryvaješ, na smich staviš ja-u roditelej už to NAROD. Vot pričina počemu ja vypustil o. Varzalija iz Eparchiji!

"Holos naroda jest holos Božij!" I NAROD, ne dľa samo chvalby sije ja hovorju, obmilki vo svojem episkopi ne zrobil. Zrobil obmilku, možlivo, o. Varzaly, dumajuči, čto episkop budet jak ovečka pokornyj jeho diktatorskim ukazam, budet pomahati jemu v roššireniji jeho Vistnika dľa jeho, o. Varzaly-a, ličnaho zarobka — "business"-a. NE o. VARZALIJU JA PRIZVAN SLUŽITI, a NARODU! S nim, s narodom ja doživaju svoji starenki dni i v objatijach svojeho milaho russkaho naroda ja želaju skončiti svoj zemnyj život. Nit! narod moj, kotoryj mene porodil i kotoroho každyj žilkoj svojeho hrišnaho tila ja iskrennu ľubľu, NE ostavit mene, jak by toho chotil o. Varzaly, že pojdet hľadati pritulisha u Moskovskich boľševikov.

Vy, oo. Redaktory, ...čto naša Eparchija ne tak plocho stojit, jak ...arzaly vo svojem "Vistniku". Odnako, m... oči na ďila našej slavnoj i Bohospasa... my živiješe pro-

---

(Prodolženije na 4-oj storoňi)

gressovati. My s Božijej pomočiju i budeme progressovati, jak skoro naš "Cerkovnyj Vistnik" zajmet misto otrovy Varzalijevskaho Vistnika.

S Archijerejskim blahoslovenijem,

† OREST
Episkop

OT REDAKCIJI

Pobožnomu karpatorusskomu narodu do jeho laskavaho vnimanija, my smirenno vručajeme siju našu jeparchiaľnuju gazetu "Cerkovnyj Vistnik."

Naš možut zapytatisja: "a čto stalosja s Varzalevskim Vistnikom?" Naš otvit: my ne znajem, ibo Varzalevskij Vistnik jest majetkom o. Varzalija. Naša učtivosť ne dozvoľajet nam mišatisja do čužich majetkov.

Odnako, my dolžny zaznačiti, čto "Varzalevskij" Vistnik spočatku byl našim Vistnikom i služil jako organ dľa našej diocezii. Tak jest! On byl našim majetkom ibo svjaščenniki osnovali jeho na svoji vlastny milodary. No neodolho stalosja tak, čto o. Varzalij bez našeho dozvolenija i bez sohlasija jeparchiaľnoj vlasti pošol do notariusa i tam nespravno prijsьhnul, čto majitelem Vistnika jest on, o. Varzalij, a ne my, i ne jeparchija. Takim sposobom naš Vistnik stalsja privatnoju novinoju o. Varzalija.

Sčilavšis' nezakonnym majitelem našeho Vistnika, o. Varzalij ne povidomil ľudej o tom, no pod plaščem našej jeparchiji prodolžal gazdovati vo svojem Vistniku na koryst svojich ličnych interesov, a imenno, vozvysiti svoju vlasť nad svjaščennikami i narodom, a takže zarobiti jak najboľše doľlarov do svojej "herojskoj" kešeni.

Po našemu nepolnomu rachunku o. Varzalij dostaval ročno ot predplatnikov na Vistnik 5 tysjačej dol., žertvy na pervovyj fond i milodary prinosili 2 tysjačej dol. Slovom — 7 tysjač. Vyťahnuvši drukarskija vydatki 4 tysjači, o. Varzalij zarabľal na svojem Vistniku 3 tysjač doľlarov ročno. Rozumijetsja, okrem Rankinskoj parafiaľnoj placy i dochodkov.

My ne zavidim nikomu, kto čestno zarabľajet na stranki, no my osuždajem tot zarobok, kotoryj prichodit inšim putem. My osuždajem fašivyja tverždenija o. Varzalija v jeho Vistniku, čto on, o. Varzalij, rabotajet dľa blaha karpatorusskaho naroda, zadarmo, daže jak by dokladajet k svojej kešeni.

My ne možem oboji molčanijem i toho žalostnoho fakta čto o. Varzalij projavľal diktatorskije sposoby nad svojimi altarnymi bratami, kohda on daval im rozskazy koľlektovati po ich parafijam na svoj Vistnik, i jesli kto vosprotivil falsja (a takovyje byli), to hrozil tomu otobrati ot neho jeho nasuščnyj chľib.

Ni v odnoj parafiji ili russkoj gazeti tut v Ameriki ne najdeš, daby odin redaktor ili izdateľ veličal sebe do neba, abo dozvoľal svojim korrespondentam toje ďilati. I s žalem i so stydom my vidim v každom Varzalevskom Vistniku jak vypučivajetsja ta osoba o. Varzalija, jak slavnoho heroja, velikoho borca, veľmožnoho monsignora i pr. Jesli by vaju Varzalijevska samochvaľbu perevesti na anglijskij jazyk i dati počitati amerikancu, to čužij nam amerikanec osudil by čitatelej takoho Vistnika, a ďiti naši han'bilsja by za nas.

(Prodolženije na 4-oj storoňi)

RUSSKIJE PRAVOSLAVNIJE CERKVI I MOSKOVSKIJ PATRIARCH.

V svojich publičnych instrukcijach po adresu našeho Vladyki Oresta, "heroj herojev" takže skazal durnicu, čto teper' vsja pravoslavnaja cerkov' objedinena i klaňajetsja Moskvi. Na samom ďili takoho ne bylo i ne jesť. To čto vysyvlajut iz Moskvy emisarov, čtoby podčiniti sebi Russkije zahraničnyje cerkvi ne uvinčalosja uspichom.

Pravda jesť, čto meždu vojnami, pervoj i druhoj, Russkije Pravoslavnyje Cerkvi ne priznavali avtoritet Moskvy. Sami oni ďijstvovali ili jak samostojateľny Cerkvi vo hlavi s Zahraničnym Sinodom v Sremskich Karlovcach ili byli pod jurisdikcijej Konstantinopoľskaho Patriarcha.

Posľi vojny tovarišč Stalin čerez svojeho Moskovskaho Patriarcha potreboval ot vsich Russkich Cerkvej pristati k Moskvi. Stareňkij Mitropolit Jevlogij vo Franciji pristal k Moskvi, no ne davno umer. V svojem zaviščaniju on naznačil svojim preemnikom Archijepiskopa Vladimira Niceskaho. Arch. Vladimir ne priznavajet Moskvy i na dňach objavil sebe zamistitelem ekzarcha. Po nanovošim višťam iz Pariža hovoritьsja, čto kosvojennyj Niceskij Vladimir, objavivšij sebja zamistitelem ekzarcha posľi smerti Mitropolita Jevlogija i otkazavšij podčinitisja Moskovskoj patriarchiji, položil odobrenije svojemu rišeniju ot Konstantinopoľskaho patriarcha, v podčineniji kotoraho arch. Vladimir i sejčas nachoditsja.

Tot že Konstantinopoľskij patriarch Maksim ne davno obmiňalsja s Mitropolitom Anastasijem po povodu svoho jeho izbranija na patriaršij prestol. V plnui k naltr. Anastasiju on posľidnaho nazyvajet "ľubeznym bratom." Značit Russkaja Cerkov Zahraničnej, kotoroj stojit v hlavi

(Prodolženije na 3-oj storoňi)

---

20. Front page of Cerkovny's *Viestnik: The Church Messenger*, vol. 1, no. 1, 1946.

21. Ecumenical Patriarch Benjamin I.

22. Bishop Orestes and Patriarch Athenagoras.

Chapter 7

"FOR I PLANTED, APOLLOS WATERED, BUT GOD GAVE THE GROWTH"

Despite the problems caused by the "Carpatho-Russian People's Church" to the diocese, the late 1940s were a time of growth. New parishes were organized or sought admission, the continuing "Latinization" of the "Byzantine Rite" (formerly Greek Catholic) Church was providing a steady stream of converts to the Orthodox faith. At this time many churches were still involved in court cases and the loss of parishes at times gave rise to almost entire congregations leaving their original church and building a new one.

150

If the growth of the diocese was to be positive and spiritually profitable it would need direction. The lack of diocesan seat, a cathedral church to serve as a gathering point, a "heart" for the diocese was becoming a liability. Bishop Orestes and the Diocesan Consistory began a search for a suitable site for a cathedral. This presented a unique set of problems.

Since the days of the "celibacy struggle," the privilege of each parish to hold its own property in trust and to manage its temporal affairs was re-affirmed in the by-laws of the diocese, even before it was Orthodox. Yet the Bridgeport experience taught the leaders of the diocese an embarassing lesson and it was resolved that the possiblity of a court case in the diocesan cathedral be totally negated by having the cathedral incorporated in the name of the diocese and any other diocesan properties associated with the cathedral.

It was of course simply not feasible to begin a new parish in an area where there were members of the diocese and it was pointless to build a cathedral where there were no members of the diocese living. The only realistic solution was for one of the parishes of the diocese to consent to becoming the cathedral to allow the cathedral church to be incorporated by the diocese. The question was which parish would consent to do this.

Johnstown Becomes the Seat of the Diocese

On October 3, 1950, Bishop Orestes announced with a special pastoral letter that Christ the Saviour Church of Johnstown had consented to become the cathedral parish of the diocese and that it was donating the land it had chosen as the site for its church and $65,000.00 that it had raised for the building of their new church.[1] The members of the Christ the Saviour parish had lost their church, Saint Mary's in the Cambria city section of Johnstown, in court to Bishop Takach's Pittsburgh Eparchy and were holding services in a former bakery. The

151

members of Christ the Saviour Church also agreed to give the use of their rectory to the dean of the cathedral or any auxillary bishop (Bishop Orestes still desired to live in Bridgeport).

An agreement to the effect of all of the above was approved by Bishop Orestes and the diocesan board of trustees and the members of the Christ the Saviour parish at a special congregational meeting on September 17, 1950. However, the parish had adopted a resolution offering its land and building fund to the diocese to be the diocesan seat at a congregational meeting in January of that year.[2]

In his pastoral letter the bishop authorized a fund drive to raise money for the building of the cathedral and praised the "noble and good-hearted Russian people of Johnstown" for their faith in the diocese and in him shown by the donation of their land and hard-earned money. The building of the cathedral, according to the bishop's letter, would be "the beginning of a new period in the history of the diocese," something that had been waited for for twelve years.[3]

"I know," he said, "that this is a great undertaking, but through deep faith one that can be completed if all, that is priests and people, work to their utmost and make sacrifices for it . . . . Let us all join our strength for the glory of God and for the good of our church and people! Let the important reminder of the Apostle Paul sound thunderously in the hearts of our priests and faithful: '. . .you know what hour it is, how it is full time for you to wake from sleep.'"(Rom. 13.11).[4]

In addition to the construction of the cathedral long term plans called for the establishment of a seminary, diocesan offices and an episcopal residence.[6]

The Johnstown parish had been the site of the last Sobor and many of the people of the diocese were familiar with the parish and its people. The A.C.R.Y. and many parishes and individuals praised the action of the

Johnstown parish and pledged their financial and moral support for the new cathedral. The construction of the cathedral became a rallying point to unify the priests and faithful of the diocese against the lingering effects of the "Varzaly schism."

A Home is Found for the Seminary

The closing days of 1950 saw the incorporation of the "Christ the Saviour Cathedral Church of the American Carpatho-Russian Orthodox Greek Catholic Diocese." But the joy surrounding the building of the cathedral was to be added to in 1951. Through the tireless efforts of Fr. John Yurcisin, the Chancellor of the diocese, the former Strayer Manor, in close proximity to the cathedral building site, was purchased by the diocese to house the Seminary on September 12, 1951.[6] Four seminarians were enrolled for the first class which met on November 2 of that year.[7]

The Dedication of the Cathedral

On July 12, 1952, the Feast of Saints Peter and Paul, the Very Rev. John Yurcisin, diocesan Chancellor and the newly-appointed pastor of the cathedral parish, broke ground for the edifice. Construction was financed by the sale of bonds to members of the diocese, the sale of which began in July of 1951 as well. The cornerstone was blessed and laid by Bishop Orestes on October 5, 1952, and the domes and crosses were blessed on July 4, 1953.

At last the construction neared completion and plans were made to celebrate the fifteenth anniversary of the diocese and the consecration of the cathedral in Johnstown. Bishop Orestes set the date for May 30, 1954. The May 15 edition of the *Church Messenger* for 1954 contained a special pastoral message from the bishop regarding the consecration of the cathedral and the diocesan anniversary celebration. He gave the following instructions to his flock: All of the priests of the diocese were to attend the Hierarchical Liturgy in the cathedral on May 30 and were given leave of their parishes for that Sunday. All of the faithful were invited and encouraged to attend but for those who could not the bishop designated the time between 11:00 and 12:00 o'clock Sunday, May 30 as a "Holy Hour" for all the faithful who could not attend the services. All of the faithful were to pray one "Our Father" and one "Hail Mary" during the "Holy Hour" "to unite their hearts and souls with Christ and with all who are praying in our Diocesan Cathedral." In addition, all church bells were to be rung at 11:00 a.m. for five minutes to herald the Holy Hour and the churches were to be open for the faithful to pray privately for the diocese and to thank Almighty God for the blessings bestowed upon the diocese and its members.[8]

Bishop Orestes had several times asked the faithful to contribute the equivalent of one day's wages to the building of the cathedral. He now asked them to join in prayer with him on the day of its dedication, to offer with him a "spiritual sacrifice," out of thanksgiving. The people of the diocese responded; over 15,000 faithful representing virtually every parish of the diocese were present for the consecration on May 30. The consecration ceremony and the Divine Liturgy were filmed by Johnstown T.V. station WJAC and the services were broadcast on radio stations WJAC and WARD of Johnstown. The choirs of Christ the Saviour Cathedral, Saint Nicholas Church of Homestead and Saint George's Church of Taylor, Pennsylvania sang the Liturgy.

Bishop Orestes issued the following solemn declaration for the consecration of the cathedral:

Episcopal Declaration

On the Occasion of The Solemn Dedication
of Christ the Saviour Cathedral

*"Be glorious and rejoice O Church of God,
for thy King cometh in all righteousness . . .
blessed art Thou having a fountain of grace,
and have mercy upon us."*

My heart overflows with joy in that Almighty and Merciful God has deigned to permit me, after forty-eight years as a Priest and fifteen years as a Bishop, to see this triumphant day come to pass. Through my humble person, your Spiritual Leader and Hierarch, we today intrust our Cathedral Church to Christ the Saviour, that all of us, Priests and Faithful of our God-preserved American Carpatho-Russian Orthodox Greek Catholic Diocese, may be UNITED THROUGH CHRIST, FOR CHRIST, AND IN CHRIST.

The Cathedral of Christ the Saviour in Johnstown, Pa., has been built by our ardent love of that same Saviour, of Whom the holy Apostle Paul wrote: "Jesus Christ, yesterday, and today, and the same forever" (Heb. 13:8). Our Cathedral will stand as a symbol and lasting monument-memorial for future generations, as a token that "Christ forever" will be with His Church and Priesthood, even as He said: "Behold I am with you all days, even to the consummation of the world" (Matth. 28:20).

My heart rejoices with "an exceeding joy" that in the Providence of God the extraordinary grace of blessing our Cathedral Church fell to me. As I gaze upon those golden domes that adorn our Sanctuary and that remind all of us

of the heavenly end of our earthly lives, I recall all that has transpired during the fifteen years of my episcopate. From a difficult beginning came years of unfortunate strife against both secret and open enemy. But then I was reminded that from the very first days of its existence, the Holy Catholic and Apostolic Church of ours has had to arm itself with patience and love for battle against those who would sow tares among the pure meadow of Apostolic teaching. Great indeed is the strength of the Church of Christ, the Orthodox and Eastern Church, and no power of darkness can shake and defame it.

Strife in our midst came to an end with the founding and building of our Christ the Saviour Cathedral. With a profound sense of gratitude, my soul is brought neigh unto Almighty God forasmuch as He deigned to have me as a participant in this great historical event. And I am equally certain that all of your feelings are saturated with sincere thanksgiving—and a "Glory be to God!"

I raise my episcopal hands this day, the Feast of Feasts of our Diocese, and from the depths of my heart come the words: "Let us lift up our hearts; let us give thanks to the Lord." We fall to our knees as the words of the Blessed Virgin Mary come to our lips: "My soul doth magnify the Lord, and my spirit hath rejoiced in God my Saviour" (Luke 1:46, 47). And thus these words have been fulfilled: "If this work was

155

not pleasing in the sight of God, we would never have been enabled to accomplish this sacred task with such remarkable progress—this task of building the Cathedral." Peace and love hath borne their fruit in this godly work!

Now, with a profound sense of gratitude I turn to our faithful Priesthood. I thank them as zealous and generous laborers in the vineyard of Christ, who have understood the significance of the Cathedral for our Diocese and for the preservation of our Carpatho-Russian Faith and Church in America, looking to a more prosperous and more glorious future for all of us.

Nor can I refrain from commenting on the sacrificial love, the magnanimity, and generosity of our beloved American Carpatho-Russian People. They readily responded with their hard-earned monies. We can well be proud of the sacrifices that Johnstown's pious people have made. Their loyalty and fidelity to their Church and Diocese will be recorded forever in the history of Holy Orthodoxy in America.

But the most significant fact is this—that our People from every part of America had a share in the building of our Cathedral Church. That is why the Cathedral is the Mother of all the Churches of our Diocese. That Cathedral is "In behalf of all and for all." From this day, the Christ the Saviour Cathedral shall be the center of the spiritual life of our God-fearing Carpatho-Russian People, the pride of our nationality, the strength of our solidarity, the pillar and affirmation of our American, Carpatho-Russian Orthodox Greek Catholic Diocese. Therefore, rejoice and be glad, O ye people, upon the occasion of this unforgetable feast! Your generous sacrifice will not be forgotten of God, but as a pure and sacred sacrifice for the sake of Christ, it shall be rewarded a hundred-fold.

The Founder and Head of our Orthodox Church is Christ Himself, in Whose Name our Cathedral has been built; its walls are the Law of God, the pillars are the Apostles, Evangelists, and teachers; its protection — the Holy Spirit Himself.

Before all else in the years to come we must support the work of our Cathedral, willingly and gladly fulfilling our obligations to it. Then with a certain hope we can await a more glorious future for our Diocese.

And in conclusion, I pray, "From the heights of Thy holiness, O Lord, look down upon Thy people waiting upon Thee, seeking from Thy hand Thy bountiful mercies; and claim all of them into Thy Kingdom."

With Fatherly Love, in Christ Jesus,

✠ ORESTES
Bishop

156

At the end of the Liturgy, Bishop Orestes presented Fr. Peter Molchany, the vicar-general of the diocese since 1938, with a mitre that had been granted by the Ecumenical Patriarchate in recognition of Fr. Molchany's years of dedication to the diocese and his work in promoting the Orthodox faith.

As Bishop Orestes noted, the building of the cathedral took place amid strife and its completion brought that strife to an end. The "Byzantine-Rite" Catholic Church through its press and the *Vistnik* of Fr. Varzaly both were critical of the building of the cathedral, expressing the opinion that it would never happen, that the money would be wasted, that Bishop Orestes was not to be trusted. May 30th silenced the critics on both sides, the dream had at last become a reality.

The First Diocesan Pilgrimage

Now that the diocese had a "spiritual center" in the cathedral and Seminary in Johnstown, emphasis was placed on renewing the spiritual life among the faithful as well as educating the young people into the Orthodox faith and their Carpatho-Russian heritage. The first diocesan pilgrimage or "Otpust" was scheduled for the cathedral and Seminary on July 2-4, 1955. This was held in conjuction with the first diocesan church school teachers conference directed by the Rev. Stephen Sedor, who authored many of the first church school materials of the diocese and who was a founding member of the Orthodox Christian Education Commission. At the "Otpust" Bishop Orestes was the main celebrant of most of the services despite his being seventy-two years of age. He also broke ground for an expansion of the Seminary, which was too small for the growing student body. The pilgrimage was an enormous success. The people of the diocese had a cause—the expansion of the Orthodox faith among Carpatho-Russian people and they had in Bishop Orestes an indefatigable

157

hierarch—their priest and spiritual father whom they loved.

The Golden Anniversary of Bishop Orestes

In the following year the faithful again gathered in Johnstown on August 26 to honor Bishop Orestes on the fiftieth anniversary of his ordination to the priesthood. Bishop Bodhan of the Ukrainian Diocese of the Ecumenical Patriarchate as well as Bishop Scaife of the Episcopal Church were in attendance at the Hierarchical Liturgy. The Cathedral Choir and the Winder Church choir sang the Liturgy after which the Bishop gave his blessing to each individual present (there were almost thousand!). At the anniversary dinner the bishop was presented with a new Mercury automobile as a gift from the priests and faithful of the diocese. The fiftieth anniversary of the Bishop received national attention in an article printed in *Newsweek* magazine. Greetings were sent to the bishop by the Ecumenical Patriarch Athenagoras.[9]

The Ministry of the Bishop in the '50s

At his fiftieth anniversary celebration Bishop Orestes was seventy-three years of age. Yet he did not dream of retiring nor could he. The 1950s saw several of the parishes that had left to join the "People's Church" return to the fold of the diocese. The year 1954 saw the first mission parish of the diocese, Saints Peter and Paul's of Levittown, Pennsylvania organized. Parishes were building, renovating and growing. The bishop was in demand almost everywhere. Despite his advanced age he insisted on driving himself to whatever part of the diocese he had to visit.

The Very Reverend Protopriest Stephen Sedor, writing at the time of the bishop's death recalled the constant trips of the bishop throughout the diocese at this time:

The matter of visits to churches was an endless task.

158

Bishop Orestes was one of the first Greek Catholic priests in this country to get an automibile. Indeed, his model A Ford, a vintage car if there was one, was a common sight on the streets of Bridgeport and Stratford for decades. There he sat solemnly in the seat, as it putted along the road.

But the long trips to parishes in Pennsylvania, Ohio, Indiana, and Illinois, called for better transportation. For this purpose, he bought a Studerbaker. It was sleek, maroon in color, with the bishop's coat-of-arms finely painted on the doors. And he had a special license plate bearing the letters OPC. Children in parishes thought it meant "official police car" until their priests would set the record straight.

The Bishop wore out one car after another in these many trips. During a visit to the Midwest in the 1950s, he spent a couple of weeks there, and then returned to Bridgeport in a 28 hour drive without overnight stop. The turnpikes weren't readily available in those days, and the journeys were long and weary.

One thing that helped break the monotony was good conversation and a good dinner. Bishop Orestes was good at the former; Howard Johnson arranged for the latter. Every meal there ended (for the bishop) with the heaping HJ strawberry shortcake. It was the tart, fresh berries that he liked.

Of course cars bring troubles. And Bishop Orestes had his share of automotive problems. One particular trip to Johnstown for a meeting was a horror. The brakes on a huge Lincoln gave out along the way, but the Bishop insisted he could make it into town. Well, he made it all right, but some hurried and pressing prayers were heard in heaven that day!

Often during these journeys, the Bishop spoke of his desire to use a helicopter for such visits. How handy it would be! Climb into one in Connecticut and then land on the parish lawn of some church in Pennsylvania or Ohio. He saw many helicopters in and around Stratford, where the Sikorsky Corporation is located. But this is one dream that never came true.

At an age when most people are in the winter of their life Bishop Orestes was enjoying himself too much watching the seeds sown through his suffering in the 1940s begin to bear fruit to even notice the chill. His was truly a "good victory."

23. Christ the Saviour Cathedral, Johnstown, Pa. The Mother Church and Spiritual Center of the American Carpatho-Russian Orthodox Greek Catholic Diocese.

24. The original Christ the Saviour Seminary building, 1951.

25. Scenes from the dedication of the Cathedral, 1954.

26. Scenes from the dedication of the Cathedral, 1954.

Chapter 8

Hold Fast to the Traditions You Were Taught By Us

However much he may have loved being with his people as their "Father in Christ," by the early 1960s the strain was beginning to show on Bishop Orestes. The 1960 Diocesan Sobor had authorized the building of an episcopal residence next to the cathedral, a residence that was destined for the use of an auxiliary bishop.[1] The residence was begun in June of 1963 and was completed by autumn of the year.

Bishop Orestes continued to be active in the diocese and took part in the C.E.O.L.A. Orthodox festival in conjunction with the A.C.R.Y. national convention that August. On September 15 1963, the diocese celebrated its twenty-fifth anniversary and, of course, Bishop Orestes, the twenty-fifth anniversary of his episcopacy. The bishop at this time explained his simple outlook that had served him so well for the past twenty-five years: "A good way to get into the good graces of God is don't ask much, but ask a little bit at a time, and gradually you will have all of it."[2] A Silver Anniversary Book was published for the affair, including a biography of the eighty years of the bishop's life as well as the history of the diocese. Despite his age, the September 30th issue of the *Church Messenger* for 1963 listed this as the bishop's schedule:

October 5, Rockaway, N.J. — Eastern Seaboard A.C.R.Y. Convention

October 6, Scranton, Pa. — Saint Nicholas Church — 25th anniversary

October 13, East Chicago, Ind. — Holy Ghost Church — blessing of new iconostasis.

Oct. 20, Freeland, Pa. — Saint Michael's Church — 25th anniversary

Oct. 27, Youngstown, Ohio — Saint Michael's Church — 25th anniversary

Nov. 10th, Phoenixville, Pa. — Holy Ghost Church — 25th anniversary

Nov. 17th, Rankin, Pa. — Saint Michael's Church — observance of patronal feast.

Nov. 24th, Warren, Ohio. Saint Nicholas Church.

This schedule would be demanding on a man half of the age of Bishop Orestes but he insisted on fulfilling it. He felt obligated as the shepherd of the flock to be in its midst as long as he was able. But by late 1963, the Bishop could not shoulder the tremendous demands placed on him by the growing diocese. He needed help.

Bishop Peter Shymansky Appointed Auxiliary

At the request of Bishop Orestes, the Ecumenical Patriachate elected Peter Shymansky, a priest formerly of the Russian Orthodox Greek Catholic Church (the

"Metropolia") auxiliary bishop on October 29, 1963. He was concecrated in the diocesan cathedral on November 21, 1963 with Bishop Orestes as a co-consecrator. Bishop Peter moved into the residence of Johnstown and was appointed by Bishop Orestes as rector of the Seminary. Bishop Orestes was still not to have peace, even with the appointment of another bishop.

Bishop Orestes Leaves Saint John the Baptist on Broadbridge Avenue

Since the loss of the Mill Hill Avenue Church in Bridgeport, Bishop Orestes, Fr. Mihaly, and a small group of people who chose to follow him had re-established their Saint John the Baptist Church in a former Roman Catholic church on Broadbridge Avenue late in 1947. Fr. Joseph Mihaly, the former seminarian of Fr. Orestes whom Bishop Takach had refused to ordain because he had married, served as the assistant pastor of the parish.

In the fall of 1963, Fr. Mihaly and several other priests of the diocese became angry with Bishop Orestes for recommending Fr. Shymanky, whom they viewed as an outsider, to the Holy Synod of the Patriarchate for consecration as bishop. Fr. Mihaly wanted another priest from within the diocese as the candidate for auxiliary.[3] At the prompting of Fr. Mihaly, the parish on Broadbridge Avenue voted not to accept the appointment of Bishop Peter.[4] Bishop Orestes thereupon refused to serve with Fr. Mihaly. The parishioners asked Bishop Orestes to continue in their church. The aged Bishop told them that this he could not do as long as Fr. Mihaly was serving there as well. Fr. Mihaly informed the congregation that he intended to remain as pastor. Bishop Orestes told Fr. Mihaly that he would not serve with him on account of his actions in attempting to block the appointment of Fr. Shymansky. He then stayed out of the Broadbridge Avenue parish and never set foot in it again.[6]

163

The December 15, 1963 issue of the *Church Messenger* carried a terse note in the "Official Announcement" column on the first page that Fr. Joseph Mihaly and two other priests who supported him were dismissed from the diocese. The Broadbridge Avenue Church was "independent" for a short time and then entered the Ukrainian Orthodox Diocese under the Ecumenical Patriarch with Fr. Mihaly remaining as its pastor.

Those who refused to follow Fr. Mihaly and chose to remain loyal to Bishop Orestes implored him to conduct services for them in his home. (The Bishop was deeply saddened by the action of the Broadbridge parish. He refused to address the congregation on the matter of Bishop Peter, feeling that they should know right from wrong. The congregation voted by a small majority to leave the diocese if Bishop Peter's nomination was not recalled—it wasn't and they did.[7]) Eventually, the bishop consented and "Saint John the Baptist Canonical Orthodox Church" in Stratford (Silver Lane) came into being with the bishop as its pastor. He loved this little church and remained officially its pastor until the day of his death.

The Death of Bishop Peter and a New Threat

After six months of promising work, Bishop Peter died suddenly on May 17, 1964. Again Bishop Orestes was called to lead the diocese. Again a new crisis threatened. Three priests of the diocese had secretly entered the Uniate Church and plans were made to set up a special jurisdiction to receive former priests of the diocese as well as parishes.[8] This jurisdiction was to be directly under Roman Catholic authorities and not under the "Byzantine-Rite" Catholic Bishops.[9] The Uniate and Catholic Churches always through the 1950s and 1960s questioned the legitimacy of the Carpatho-Russian Orthodox Diocese and in general found it a thorn in the side, since it was at this time that the Uniate "Byzantine-Rite" Catholic Church was Latinizing itself heavily; the Carpatho-Russian

Orthodox Diocese reminded it too much of its recent past.

Court cases were instituted in several churches of the diocese. All of the court cases ended favorably for the diocese except one, the guilty priests dismissed and the threat brought to an end.[10]

The Arrival of Bishop Methodios

In February of 1965, Bishop Methodios Kanchuha, the Orthodox auxiliary Bishop of Mihalovce in Czechoslovakia came to the United States after attending a Pan-Orthodox Conference in Rhodes. The Ecumenical Patriarch approved him as the auxiliary bishop of the Carpatho-Russian Diocese and he was installed and functioned through the spring and summer of 1965. The Czechoslovakian Orthodox Church refused to grant him a canonical release and the Ecumenical Patriarch, at the request of that Church, asked that he return to Czechoslovakia, which he did.

Bishop Orestes Elevated to Metropolitan

On December 23, 1965, the diocesan chancery office was notified that Bishop Orestes had been elevated to the rank of metropolitan by the Holy Synod of the Ecumenical Patriarchate for his twenty-seven years of service to the diocese and his service to the Orthodox Church in general. He was installed by Archbishop Iakovos at the Greek Orthodox Archdiocesan Cathedral in New York on January 1, 1966. Commenting on his elevation, Metropolitan Orestes said: "This honor which I have been accorded as a humble person is also a great honor for our diocese, our clergy, and our people."[11] The ceremony was attended by many of the clergy and faithful of the Eastern Pennsylvania and the New York Metropolitan area parishes.

Bishop John Martin Becomes Auxiliary Bishop

The health of Metropolitan Orestes began to fail early in 1966 requiring his hospitalization from time to time.

An auxiliary bishop was needed urgently. On the recommendation of Metropolitan Orestes, the Very Rev. John Martin, a brilliant and dynamic young priest, a convert to Orthodoxy from the Byzantine Rite Catholic Church and formerly its Chancellor, was elected by the Holy Synod of the Ecumenical Patriarchate to be titular bishop of Nyssa and appointed auxiliary bishop of the diocese on August 16, 1966. He was consecrated in Christ the Saviour Cathedral by Archbishop Iakovos, Metropolitan Orestes, and Bishop Theophilos with hundreds in attendance on October 6, 1966. The reaction of the eighty-three year old Metropolitan Orestes: "Now I'll be able to sleep easier at night."

27. Bishop Peter Shymansky (1963-1964).

28. Bishop Methodios Kanchuha (1965).

29. Metropolitan Orestes bestowing the rank of Archimandrite upon Fr. John Martin prior to his consecration as Bishop in September 4, 1966 at old St. George's Church, Taylor, Pa.

30. Bishop John Martin (1966-1984).

31. The new Diocesan Administration Building and Bishop's Residence.

32. Liturgy in the Cathedral.

Chapter 9

You Are a Priest Forever, According to the Order of Melchisedek

---

With the presence of Bishop John at the helm of the diocese, Metropolitan Orestes began to enter more and more into a retired life. He served in the little church in Stratford that was founded on love for him, being assisted by a newly ordained priest. Each year the members of the Stratford parish presented him with a bouquet of roses, one for each year of his long life. As his health began to fail a parishioner, Mr. Paul Dolyak, took up residence with the Bishop to help him.

The Diocese Celebrates the Metropolitan's 30th Anniversary as Bishop

On November 10, 1968, members of the clergy and faithful of the diocese gathered at Saint Michael's Church in Binghamton, New York to celebrate the thirtieth anniversary of Metropolitan Orestes' consecration. Bishop John and Fr. Vicar Peter Molchany, the vicar-general of the diocese, led the celebration which was attended by a huge crowd. Following the celebration of the Divine Liturgy there was a testimonial banquet in Saint Michael's Recreation Center, seating a thousand people. Bishop John, in the main address spoke of the Metropolitan's spirituality with these words, "His Eminence always looks up and forward to God. In many conversations with His Eminence, it has amazed me the vast spiritual reservoir he possesses. In asking him what sustains him in his faith, amid numerous problems, he replied, 'You'll always have problems as long as you live. You chose to follow Christ.' "[1]

In responding to all of the messages of the day, Metropolitan Orestes, now eighty-five years old, did not speak for any length of time. He offered these words to his followers: "My love for you is without any barrier. I thank you."[2]

The Last Days of Metropolitan Orestes

The thirtieth anniversary was a memorable event in the life of the metropolitan and in the diocese. Metropolitan Orestes continued to make public appearances from time to time as his health permitted. He was always keenly interested in the affairs of the diocese.

In 1971, the Bridgeport Mill Hill Avenue parish, which had left the diocese and Bishop Orestes twenty-five years earlier, voted overwhelmingly to leave the "Russian Metropolia" which had accepted it and return to the fold of Metropolitan Orestes' Carpatho-Russian Orthodox Diocese.

In 1974, Paul Dolyak, who had been taking care of the Metropolitan during his frequent bouts with illness passed away. Fr. John and Pani Duranko of the Mill Hill Avenue parish opened up their hearts and the spacious Mill Hill rectory to the Metropolitan and took him into their own home, making the last years of his life brighter with their love and that of their children for the aged hierarch.

The Metropolitan still, as much as he was able, took interest in diocesan affairs though he could no longer travel. He always enjoyed seeing the seminarians of the diocese each Lent as they made their annual trip to the Bridgeport parish and more than once told them "because of you the diocese will never die!"

On February 17, 1977 after a period of illness, Metropolitan Orestes finished his race, he passed on into the presence of the Lord whom he had so faithfully served throughout the ninety-three years of his life, his seventy years as a priest, and thirty-eight years as a bishop. He had at least achieved the "Good Victory."

The Funeral of Metropolitan Orestes

On Saturday, February 19, 1977, the body of Metropolitan Orestes was placed in state in the Stratford Church that he had loved so much. That evening Bishop John celebrated with local clergy the first half of the "Office for the Burial of a Priest." On Sunday morning, February 20, Bishop John celebrated the Liturgy with Fr. Richard Scott, the pastor of Saint John the Baptist Church in Stratford with the body of the Metropolitan lying in state. That afternoon the body was carried in solemn procession to Saint John the Baptist Church on Mill Hill Avenue. At 8:00 P.M. the priests of the diocese, with many other local Orthodox clergy, began to chant the second half of the priest's funeral office together with Bishop John.

On Monday, February 20, at 10:00 A.M., Bishop John, in the presence of numerous Orthodox hierarchs from the Greek Archdiocese, the Orthodox Church in

America, and the Ukrainian Diocese, began the celebration of the Divine Liturgy that the Metropolitan loved so much. The interior of the enormous Mill Hill Avenue Church was filled to standing room only. Many people shed tears on viewing the earthly remains of the man that they knew as "Bishop," then "Metropolitan" but first as "Father in Christ."

His Excellency Bishop John in his eulogy for the Metropolitan cited examples from the Scriptures of how in times of trouble God had always raised up great prophets, kings and leaders to guide his people. "The Life of Metropolitan Orestes," he said, "is proof to us that a good man does make a difference. Great men in all periods of history have proved that their zeal and knowledge and dedication changed the ebb and flow of life during their times. Metropolitan Orestes was such a person . . . He is a legend in his own time."

The Bishop went on, saying, "Like the fishermen Andrew and Peter whom Christ called first, the Metropolitan was physically robust. Like Peter and Andrew he had a simple faith and an easy manner. Like those Apostles he had a strength of spirit to live and to die a martyrdom for the teachings of the Church as Christ founded it. Like them also, he was called to be a bishop and a father of people: 'Andrew of Greece, Peter of Antioch, Orestes of the Carpatho-Russians.' "

Referring to the Metropolitan's love for the liturgical ceremonies of the Orthodox Church, Bishop John drew comparison to the Old Testment High Priest Simon mentioned in the Book of Sirach (50.11): "When he put on his glorious robe and clothed himself with the perfection of power and went up to the holy altar, he honored the vesture of holiness."

The Bishop continued, "I pray that what I have learned from the life of the Metropolitan—his reliance of God, his human touch, his quiet acceptance of reality, his resignation to life itself—might to some small degree be reflected in my own life, like the moon reflects the light of the sun."

Asking the hundreds in attendance to pray for the Metropolitan, Bishop John quotod tho Lcttcr to the Hebrews: "Remember your prelates who first spoke God's message to you; and reflecting on the outcome of their life and work, follow the example of their faith" (Hebrews 13.7).

The body of the Metropolitan was laid to rest in the cemetery of Saint John the Baptist Church of Mill Hill Avenue in Bridgeport as the priests of the diocese sang the prayer "Vicnaja pamjat"—"Eternal memory."

33. His Eminence, the Most Reverend Orestes P. Chornock, D.D., Titular Metropolitan of Agathonikeia, Bishop of the American Carpatho-Russian Orthodox Greek Catholic Diocese.

34. His Eminence Metropolitan Orestes with the Most Reverend John R. Martin, D.D., Titular Bishop of Nyssa and Auxiliary Bishop of the Diocese.

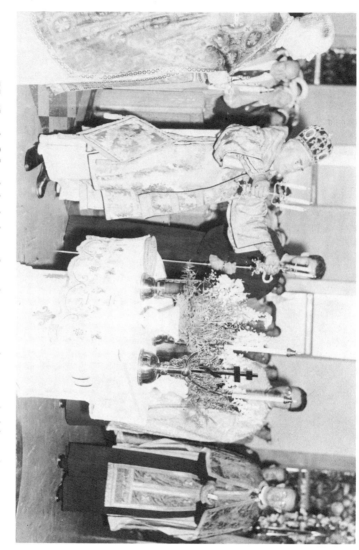

35. "Lord, O Lord, look down from heaven and see, and visit and bless his vineyard . . . ."

36. Bishop Orestes on his Golden Anniversary.

Chapter 10

The Legacy of Metropolitan Orestes

The "Good Victory" obtained by Metropolitan Orestes lives on today in the American Carpatho-Russian Orthodox Greek Catholic Diocese. The A.C.R.Y. organization that he loved so much is still carrying out the tasks that he instructed it in, working for a greater awareness of the Orthodox faith and a greater practice of Orthodox spirituality among its members and the diocese as a whole; keeping alive an awareness of the Carpatho-Russian roots of the founders of the diocese.

The Metropolitan's love of young people went beyond just the A.C.R.Y. He was instrumental in setting up the "Alpha-Omega" award for the Boy Scouts of the diocese and for all Orthodox scouts in 1956. In 1957 he authorized the first diocesan Altar Boy's retreat at the Seminary in Johnstown, under the direction of Frs. Stephen Dutko and John Dolhy, who have been conducting the retreats to encourage vocations to the priesthood ever since.

Metropolitan Orestes was proud of the Seminary in Johnstown and visited often to give examinations (many priests still recall his "thought provoking questions!") which he conducted orally. The Seminary was authorized by the State of Pennsylvania to grant a Bachelor of Theology degree in 1960. Over 100 students have attended and graduated with almost 98% becoming priests in the Orthodox Church, two becoming bishops.

The Metropolitan himself ordained fifty-five men to the holy priesthood of the Orthodox Church. He loved his priests and even when individuals strayed, he was always ready to forgive if they were repentant. Through them his ministry continues to this day.

The ancient Fathers of the Desert considered a "theologian" as "someone who prays" and in that sense Metropolitan Orestes was a brilliant theologian. His was no "textbook" theology that was learned in an armchair but a theology born out of personal suffering and sacrifices made on the altar of life. His "theological system" is expressed by the Apostle Paul in his letter to the Romans, "Do not be overcome by evil, overcome evil with good." (Romans 12.21). Those who lived with the Metropolitan recall that throughout his life he never spoke evil of his enemies or those who hurt him. His eyes were never on the injuries of the past but on the possibilities held by the future.

He struggled to overcome evil with good and his "good victory" is our lasting Orthodox heritage.

NOTES

CHAPTER ONE

[1] J. D. Douglas, e.d., *The New International Dictionary of the Christian Church* (Michigan, 1974), p. 299.

[2] S. V. Bulgakov, *Nastolnaja Kniha* (Charchov 1900), p. 407.

[3] Golden Jubilee of the Most Reverend Orestes P. Chornock, D.D. (Johnstown, Pa.: The American Carpatho-Russian Orthodox Greek Catholic Diocese, 1956), p.9.

[4] Except for "Carpatho-Ukraine" in 1939.

[5] Distinct from White Russia (Byelo-Rus') and Great Russia (Velikij Rus'), also known as Little Russia (Malij Rus').

[6] Dr. Simeon Pysh, *A Short History of Carpatho-Russia*, trans. Andrew J. Yurkovsky (Andrew J. Yurkovsky, 1973), p. 8.

[7] Very Rev. Msgr. John Yurcisin, *A History of the Carpatho-Russian People and Their Church* (Unpublished Manuscript, 1974), p.71.

[8] Ibid.

[9] Ibid.

[10] Paul R. Magocsi, *The Rusyn-Ukrainians of Czechoslovakia* (Vienna, 1983), p. 31.

[11] Yurcisin, *A History of the Carpatho-Russian People*, p. 12.

[12] Magocsi, *The Rusyn-Ukrainians of Czechoslovakia*, p. 12.

[13] Francis Dvornik, *Byzantine Missions Among the Slavs* (New Brunswick, 1970), p. 194.

[14] Donald Attwater, *The Christian Churches of the East* (Milwaukee, 1961), p. 88.

[15] Magocsi, *The Rusyn-Ukrainians of Czechoslovakia*, p. 12.

[16] Feast Day, July 26.

[17] Panagia is a ritual, elevating a triangular particle of bread in honor of the Mother of God at the refectory.

[18]Yurcisin, *A History of the Carpatho-Russian People*, p. 75.
[19]Rev. Joseph P. Hanulya, *Rusin Literature* (Cleveland, 1941), p. 18.
[20]Ibid., pp. 18, 21.
[21]Ibid., p. 18.
[22]Magocsi, *The Rusyn-Ukrainians of Czechoslovakia*, p. 14.
[23]Ibid., p. 15.
[24]Dvornik, *Byzantine Missions Among the Slavs*, pp. 164-65.
[25]Memories of the Fourth Crusade of 1204 still made most Byzantines suspicious of the West.
[26]Georges Florovsky, *Ways of Russian Theology* (Belmont, Ma., 1979), 5, chapter 2.
[27]Ibid., p. 55.
[28]Ibid., p. 56.
[29]Greek Rite is now called "Byzantine."
[30]Magocsi, *The Rusyn-Ukrainians of Czechoslovakia*, p. 15.
[31]Ibid.
[32]Warzeski, *Byzantine Rite Rusins in Carpatho-Ruthenia and America*, pp. 35, 36.
[33]Yurcisin, *A History of the Carpatho-Russian People*, pp. 85, 86.
[34]Ibid.
[35]Warzeski, *Byzantine Rite Rusins in Carpatho-Ruthenia and America*, p. 36.
[36]Yurcisin, *A History of the Carpatho-Russian People*, p. 80.
[37]Ibid.
[38]Ibid.
[39]Ibid.
[40]Wareski, *Byzantine Rite Rusins in Carpatho-Ruthenia and America*, p. 35.
[41]Magocsi, *The Rusyn-Ukrainians of Czechoslovakia*, p. 15.
[42]Very Rev. John Yurcisin, Rev. Stephen Sedor, and Rt. Rev. Mitered Peter E. Molchany, *Christ the Savior Cathedral Dedication Commemorative Book Fifteenth Diocesan Anniversary* (Johnstown, Pa.: American Carpatho-Russian Orthodox Greek Catholic Diocese, 1954), p. 24.

[43]Magocsi, *The Rusyn-Ukrainians of Czechoslavakia,* p. 61, note 42.

[44]"The Persecution and Death of Father Maxim Sandovich," *Orthodox Life,* 29, No. 4 (July-August 1979) 18-22.

[45]Yurcisin, Sedor, and Molchany, *Christ the Saviour Cathedral Dedication,* p. 14.

[46]Meletius Michael Solovey, *The Byzantine Divine Liturgy,* trans. Demetrius Emil Wysoc Hansky (Washington, D.C., 1970), p. 88.

[47]Ibid.

[48]Alexander Duchnovich, *The History of the Eparchy of Prjasev,* trans. Athanasius B. Pekar (Rome, 1971), p. 102.

[49]Oscar Jaszi, *The Dissolution of the Hapsburg Monarchy* (Chicago, 1964), p. 391.

[50]Yurcisin, *A History of the Carpatho-Russian People,* p. 84.

[51]Athanasius Pekar, *Historical Background of the Eparchy of Prjashev* (Pittsburgh, 1968), p. 26.

[52]Rev. Stephen Sedor, ed., *The A.C.R.Y. Annual 1959* (Pittsburgh: Slavia Printing Company, Inc., 1959), 9, p. 58.

[53]Paul R. Magocsi, *The Shaping of a National Identity* (Cambridge, 1979), p. 179.

[54]Dr. Richard Renoff, *Seminary Background and the Carpatho-Russian Celibacy Schism* Fairview, N.J.: The Carpatho-Russian Research Center), p. 56.

[55]Ibid.

[56]Sedor, *The A.C.R.Y. Annual 1959,* p. 61.

CHAPTER TWO

[1] Paul Robert Magocsi, "Carpatho-Rusyns," in Stephan Thernstrom, ed., *Harvard Encyclopedia of American Ethnic Groups* (Cambridge, 1980), p. 200.

[2] Ibid.

[3] Paul R. Magocsi, *The Rusyn-Ukrainians of Czechoslovakia* (Vienna: Novrographic, 1983), p. 31.

[4] Ibid., p. 30.

[5] Walter C. Warzeski, *Byzantine Rite Rusins in Carpatho-Ruthenia and America* (Pittsburgh, 1971), p. 97.

[6] Ibid.

[7] Ibid., p. 96.

[8] John Slivka, *Historical Mirror: Sources of the Rusin and Hungarian Greek Rite Catholics in the United States of America 1884-1963* (Brooklyn, 1978), p. 3.

[9] Ibid.

[10] Ibid.

[11] Either Union of Uzhorod or of Brest-Litovsk.

[12] Slivka, *Historical Mirror*, p. 3.

[13] Ibid.

[14] Ibid.

[15] Foraneus, "Some Thoughts on the Ruthenian Question in the United States and Canada," *The Ecclesiastical Review*, 52 (January 1915) 46.

[16] Ibid., p. 49.

[17] Ibid., p. 50.

[18] Very Rev. Msgr. John Yurcisin, *A History of the Carpatho-Russian People and their Church* (Unpublished Manuscript, 1974), p. 156.

[19] Slivka, *Historical Mirror*, pp. 6-7.

[20] Ibid.

[21] Constance J. Tarasar, ed., *Orthodox America 1794-1976* (Syosset, N.Y., 1980), p. 51.

[22] George Soldatow, ed., *Archpriest Alexis Toth, Volume One, Letters, Articles, Papers, and Sermons* (Canada: Synaxis Press, 1978), p. 24.

[23] Ibid.

[24] Slivka, *Historical Mirror*, p. 8.

[25] Ibid.

[26] Magocsi, *The Rusyn Ukrainians of Czechoslovakia*, p. 42.

[27] Soldatow, *Archpriest Alexis Toth*, p. 28.

[28] Slivka, *Historical Mirror*, p. 21.

[29] Ibid., p. 22.

[30]Warzeski, *Byzantine Rite Rusins*, p. 110.

[31]Ibid.

[32]Ibid.

[33]Slivka, *Historical Mirror*, p. 51, A. R. Viestnik, April 18, 1907.

[34]Ibid., p. 52, paragraph 4.

[35]Warzeski, *Byzantine Rite Rusins*, p. 121.

[36]Ibid., p. 122.

[37]Ibid., p. 123.

[38]Yurcisin, *A History of the Carpatho-Russian People*, p. 178.

[39]Warzeski, *Byzantine Rite Rusins*, p. 124.

CHAPTER THREE

[1] John Slivka, *Historical Mirror Sources of the Rusin and Hungarian Greek Rite Catholics in the United States of America 1884-1963* (Brooklyn, 1978), p. 87.

[2] Much of the material taken from personal interviews and reflections on him by persons who knew him well.

[3] "Cantors" at this time did not just lead the singing in the church but had several responsibilities including teaching Church School, Russian school, producing theatrical works, and teaching music.

[4] Walter C. Warzeski, *Byzantine Rite Rusins in Carpatho-Ruthenia and America* (Pittsburgh, 1971), p. 198.

[5] Slivka, *Historical Mirror*, p. 185.

[6] Dr. Richard Renoff, *Seminary Background and the Carpatho-Russian Celibacy Schism* (Fairview, N.J.:The Carpatho-Rusyn Research Center), p. 60.

[7] Ibid.

CHAPTER FOUR

[1] Walter C. Warzeski, *Byzantine Rite Rusins in Carpatho-Ruthenia and America* (Pittsburgh, 1971), p. 207.

[2] John Slivka, *Historical Mirror Sources of the Rusin and Hungarian Greek Rite Catholics in the United States of America 1884-1963* (Brooklyn, 1978), p. 187, pamphlet of 1932

[3] Ibid.

[4] Very Rev. Msgr. John Yurcisin, *A History of the Carpatho-Russian People and their Church* (Unpublished Manuscript, 1974), p. 192.

[5] See text, Slivka, *Historical Mirror*, p. 130.

[6] Ibid., p. 186.

[7] Ibid.

[8] Slivka, *Historical Mirror*, p. 153.

[9] Ibid., p. 1.

[10] Warzeski, *Byzantine Rite Rusins*, p. 208.

[11] Ibid., p. 211.

[12] Ibid., p. 207.

[13] Pastoral Letter 115, February 28, 1928.

[14] Pastoral Letter 80, June 12, 1931.

[15] *A.R.V.*, June 25, 1931.

[16] Basil Shereghy, *Bishop Basil Takach "The Good Shepherd"* (Pittsburgh, 1979), p. 43.

[17] Slivka, *Historical Mirror*, Minutes of clergy conference August 1933, p. 202.

[18] Ibid., p. 150.

[19] Ibid.

[20] Slivka, *Historical Mirror*, p. 143, "Brief before Metropolitan Tribunal," 1931.

[21] Ibid.

[22] Ibid.

[23] Slivka, *Historical Mirror*, p. 187, pamphlet of 1932.

[24] Ibid.

[25] Ibid.

[26] Ibid.

[27] Pastoral Letter 66, May 18, 1931.

[28] Slivka, *Historical Mirror*, p. 148, brief of Defendant.

[29] Ibid.

[30]Pastoral Letter, July 15, 1932.

[31]Slivka, *Historical Mirror*, p. 157.

[32]Sacred Congregation for Eastern Rites Protocol Number 572, 1932.

[33]Slivka, *Historical Mirror*, p. 203, Clergy minutes, 1933.

[34]Ibid., p. 174, Minutes K.O.V.O.

[35]Ibid., p. 135, Minutes G.C.U.

[36]Ibid., p. 176.

[37]Ibid.

[38]See text in Slivka, *Historical Mirror*, pp. 181-92.

[39]Ibid.

[40]Ibid.

[41]Warzeski, *Byzantine Rite Rusins*, p. 225.

[42]Ibid.

[43]*Vostok*, Twenty-fifth Anniversary Commemorative Edition, p. 5.

[44]Slivka, *Historical Mirror*, p. 287.

[45]Yurcisin, *A History of the Carpatho-Russian People*, p. 195.

[46]*A.R.V.* July 27, 1933, p. 3. "Kto Jest Episkop Bucis?"

[47]*A.R.V.* February 2, 1933, p. 7.

[48]*A.R.V.* June 1, 1933, p. 1.

[49]"Rusin Church Congress," *Johnstown Tribune*, June 12, 1933.

[50]*A.R.V.* June 15, 1933, p. 1.

[51]Slivka, *Historical Mirror*, p. 196.

[52]Ibid.

[53]Ibid.

[54]Pastoral Letter 116, June 28, 1933.

[55]Slivka, *Historical Mirror*, p. 200.

[56]*A.R.V.* August 3, 1932.

[57]Slivka, *Historical Mirror*, p. 212.

[58]See Chapter 2.

[59]Slivka, *Historical Mirror*, p. 203.

[60]Ibid., p. 204.

[61]Ibid., pp. 204-05.

[62]Ibid., p. 208.

[63]Ibid.

[64]Ibid., p. 209.

[65]Ibid.

[66]Ibid.,p. 210.

[67]Ibid.

[68]Ibid., p. 215.

[69]*A.R.V.* August 24, 1933, p. 7, "Sblizujetsja Cas Konecnoho Racunka."

[70]Warzeski, *Byzantine Rite Rusins,* p. 210.

[71]Ibid.

[72]Ibid., p. 209.

[73]*A.R.V.* January 12, 1933, "G.C.U. 100% Procentov Solventnoje."

[74]For instance, a committee was supposed to visit Bishop Takach and give his reply at the 1933 National Church Congress; see Slivka, *Historical Mirror,* p. 200.

[75]*A.R.V.* June 6, 1933, p. 1.

[76]*A.R.V.* September 28, 1933, p. 7.

[77]See text of "Our Stand" in Slivka, *Historical Mirror,* p. 257.

[78]See text in Michael Roman, *Golden Jubilee 1892-1942* (Munhall, Pa.: G.C.U. Printing Company, 1942), pp. 372-74.

[79]Slivka, *Historical Mirror,* p. 266, "Our Stand."

[80]Ibid.

[81]The Synod of Zamosc, held in 1720, approved the following "Latinizations" for the "United" (i.e. "Uniate") Church: substitution of the amice and alb for the sticharion, placing of the antimension between the two altar covers instead of folded in the eiliton, the elimination of the "Zeon" or "Teplota," the elimination of the "sponge," the "Filioque."

[82]*A.R.V.* September 26, 1935, pp. 6-7.

[83]Pastoral Letter 291, 1935.

[84]*Vistnik* March 5, 1936, p. 1.

[85]Pastoral Letter 37, 1935.

[86]*Vistnik* February 27, 1936, p. 1. However he did not return

to the A.R.V. until July 1936, when he was re-elected by the G.C.U. Convention.

[87]Yurcisin, *A History of the Carpatho-Russian People*, p. 209.

[88]Ibid., p. 209.

[89]*Vistnik*, February 27, 1936, p. 3.

[90]Ibid. This had been a point of contention between Bishop Takach and the opposition.

[91]Ibid., p. 2, not to be confused with the A.R.V.

In later years (1959) Fr. Hanulya, who though fiercely "anti-celibacy," yet who was unwilling to risk suspension by Bishop Takach for his belief, stated in an interview that Fr. Orestes Chornock was to be the figurehead for a group of clergymen who sought to wrest control of the diocese of Pittsburgh. These priests lured (according to Hanulya) Fr. Orestes Chornock into the group with the promise that he would be the bishop since he was a widower and eligible. The excommunications that proceeded out of the organization of the new Greek Catholic diocese then supposedly frightened off the group who left Fr. Orestes and a few others to continue alone. Fr. Hanulya must have confused his facts.

Fr. Orestes Chornock and five other priests were excommunicated *nominatum,* as we shall see, by Pius XI on October 17, 1936, confirming the proceedings of the Eparchial Tribunal of May 27, 1936. Pani Yolanda Chornock did not pass away until May 28, 1937, a year and a day *after* Fr. Orestes had been excommunicated by Bishop Takach's tribunal and almost eight months after the nominatum excommunication by the pope. At the time he was elected Administrator of the new diocese (February 4, 1936), Fr. Orestes *was not eligible for the episcopacy* and would not have been for well over a year. By the time of the "National Religious Congress" of November 1937, which elected Fr. Orestes as bishop of the "Carpatho-Russian Greek Catholic Diocese of the Eastern Rite," he had in fact been excommunicated (nominatum) from the Roman Church for over a year and had broken all ties with it since May of 1936, two months after his installation as administrator upon which he responded to Bishop Takach in a letter.

[92]*Vistnik*, February 27, 1936, p. 1.

[93]See page 65.

182

[94]*Vistnik,* February 27, 1936, p. 1.

[95]*Vistnik,* March 5, 1936, p. 1.

[96]Ibid., p. 2.

[97]*Vistnik,* February 27, 1936, 1:1, p. 3.

[98]Ibid., p. 1.

[99]Article reprinted on p. 3, *Vistnik* March 12, 1936, 1:3.

[100]Article reprinted in *Vostok* March 19, 1936, 16:385, p. 6.

[101]Personal interview with Very Rev. Msgr. John Yurcisin, July 22, 1984.

[102]Warzeski, *Byzantine Rite Rusins,* p. 221.

[103]Slivka, *Historical Mirror,* p. 288.

[104]*Vistnik,* 1:21, July 30, 1936, p. 3.

[105]Ibid., p. 4. Article reprinted from *Wilkes-Barre Record* July 2, 1936.

[106]Ibid. Reprinted article from *Wilkes-Barre Evening News.*

[107]Ibid., p. 1.

[108]Ibid., p. 4. Reprinted article from the *Wilkes-Barre Evening News.*

[109]*A.R.V.* August 20, 1936.

[110]Text in Slivka, *Historical Mirror,* p. 300.

[111]*Vistnik,* 1:30, October 1, 1936, p. 1.

[112]Ibid.

[113]See letters of Fr. Toth, Soldatow, *Archpriest Alexis Toth.*

[114]Yurcisin, *A History of the Carpatho-Russian People,* p. 198.

[115]Ibid.

[116]It was not because of concern for Greek immigrants as one apologist for "American Orthodoxy" has stated, but rather for ex-Uniates whose national, as well as spiritual, identity caused them to continue to refer to themselves as Greek Catholics.

[117]This was being done in Europe as well, as early as 1929.

[118]Pastoral Letter 225, November 25, 1936. Ironically the akathist to the "Sacred Heart" was one of the "Latinizations" Bishop Takach was accused of.

[119]All following references are found in the minutes of the Congress of November 1937, on file in the chancery office of the American Carpatho-Russian Orthodox Greek Catholic

Diocese, Johnstown, Pennsylvania.

[120]Ibid.

[121]Ibid.

[122]Personal interview with Very Rev. Protopriest John Yurcisin on March 11, 1985.

[123]Congress of November 1937 minutes.

[124]Ibid.

[125]Slivka, *Historical Mirror*, p. 170, "Minutes from the K.O.V.O."

[126]Paul R. Magocsi, *Our People* (Toronto, Canada: Multicultural History Society of Ontario, 1984), p. 24.

[127]Tarasar, *Orthodox America 1794-1976*, p. 92.

[128]Ibid., p. 132.

[129]Yurcisin, *A History of the Carpatho-Russian People*, p. 180.

[130]Tarasar, *Orthodox America 1794-1976*, p. 183.

[131]Ibid.

[132]Johann von Gardner, "A Few Words on Church Chant in Carpatho-Russia," *Orthodox Life*, 30, No. 1 (1980) 49.

[133]See note 81.

[134]Jaroslav Roman, "The Establishment of the American Carpatho-Russian Orthodox Greek Catholic Diocese in 1938: A Major Carpatho-Russian Uniate Return to Orthodoxy," *St. Vladimir's Theological Quarterly*, 20 (1976), p. 158.

[135]Personal interview with the Rt. Rev. Mitered Peter E. Molchany, Vicar-General of the American Carpatho-Russian Orthodox Greek Catholic Diocese, August 12, 1983 at Homestead, Pennsylvania.

[136]Yurcisin, *A History of the Carpatho-Russian People*, p. 212.

[137]Ibid., p. 214.

CHAPTER FIVE

[1] All of the information presented was taken from the official minutes of the conference on file at the chancery office of the American Carpatho-Russian Orthodox Greek Catholic Diocese in Johnstown, Pennsylvania.

[2] Ibid.

[3] Very Rev. Msgr. John Yurcisin, "A History of the A.C.R.Y.," *American Carpatho-Russian Youth Annual* (Pittsburgh, 1970), p. 146.

[4] *Silver Anniversary Commemorative Book* of the American Carpatho-Russian Orthodox Greek Catholic Diocese of the U.S.A. (Johnstown, 1963), p. 43.

[5] Minutes of the Second Diocesan Sobor (1940) on file at the chancery office in Johnstown.

[6] Warzeski, *Byzantine Rite Rusins*, p. 219.

[7] Sheregy, *Bishop Basil Takach*, p. 48.

[8] Warzeski, *Byzantine Rite Rusins*, p. 241.

[9] Ibid.

CHAPTER SIX

[1] Yurcisin, *A History of the Carpatho-Russian People*, p. 220.

[2] Ibid.

[3] Ibid., p. 221.

[4] *The Church Messenger* (September 19, 1946) 4.

[5] Ibid., 3.

[6] Ibid.

[7] Ibid., 1.

[8] The following references are from the official minutes of the Third Diocesan Sobor (1946) on file in the chancery office in Johnstown, Pennsylvania.

[9] Minutes of the Fourth Diocesan Sobor (1947) on file in the chancery office in Johnstown, Pennsylvania.

[10] Personal interview with Mr. John Kamenitsky, on June 20, 1983 in Stratford, Connecticut.

[11] Ibid.

[12] Ibid.

[13] 1947, (Fourth) Diocesan Sobor Minutes.

[14] 1970, A.C.R.Y. Annual, p. 151.

[15] Ibid. The full text of the resolution is printed in the 1970 A.C.R.Y. Annual on p. 152.

[16] 1947, Diocesan Sobor Minutes.

[17] *The Church Messenger* (December 15, 1947) 1 for the full text.

[18] Idem (September 15, 1949) 2 for the text.

CHAPTER SEVEN

[1] *The Church Messenger* (October 15, 1950) for the full text.

[2] Yurcisin, *A History of the Carpatho-Russian People,* p. 229.

[3] *The Church Messenger* (October 15, 1950).

[4] Ibid.

[5] Ibid.

[6] Yurcisin, *A History of the Carpatho-Russian People,* p. 230.

[7] Ibid., p. 231.

[8] *The Church Messenger* (May 15, 1954) 1 for the full text.

[9] For more details see *The Church Messenger* (October 31, 1956).

CHAPTER EIGHT

[1] Yurcisin, *A History of the Carpatho-Russian People,* p. 237.

[2] *The Church Messenger* (September 30, 1963).

[3] Personal interview with John Kamenitsky, on June 20, 1983 in Stratford, Connecticut.

[4] Ibid.

[5] Ibid.

[6] Ibid.

[7] Ibid.

[8] Yurcisin, *A History of the Carpatho-Russian People,* p. 239.

[9] Ibid.

[10] Ibid., p. 239. See also the 1965 Diocesan Sobor minutes for the principals.

[11] *The Church Messenger* (December 30, 1965).

CHAPTER NINE

[1]*The Church Messenger* (November 24, 1968) 3.
[2]Ibid.
[3]Ibid., August 8, 1971.
[4]Ibid., February 27, 1977.